SUICIDE OF A NATION

This book is dedicated to
the Forgotten Majority.

MATT GOODWIN

SUICIDE OF A NATION

IMMIGRATION, ISLAM, IDENTITY

First published in 2026 by Northstar
mattgoodwin.org
Copyright © Matt Goodwin, 2026
Updated second edition

EU GPSR Authorised Representative
LOGOS EUROPE, 9 rue Nicolas Poussin, 17000,
LA ROCHELLE, France
E-mail: Contact@logoseurope.eu

ISBN 978-1-9194014-0-9
Also available as an eBook
ISBN 978-1-9194014-1-6
and as an Audiobook
ISBN 978-1-9194014-2-3

Edited by Richard Collins
Designed and typeset by Typo•glyphix
Cover design by Michal Kuzmierkiewicz
Project management by Whitefox
Printed and bound by 4edge Ltd

CONTENTS

ABOUT THIS BOOK

Many of the arguments in this book draw on data and information I have collected and analysed in my online Substack newsletter: mattgoodwin.org

At the time of writing, nearly 100,000 people read our newsletter each day. You can join us via the website above or the QR code below.

ABOUT THE AUTHOR

Matt Goodwin is a writer, academic and media commentator. He has written seven books including two *Sunday Times* national bestsellers, *National Populism: The Revolt Against Liberal Democracy* (2018) and *Values, Voice and Virtue: The New British Politics* (2023). An earlier book was longlisted for the Orwell Prize. Matt was a university academic for twenty years and Professor of Politics. He is Honorary Professor at the University of Kent, Senior Research Fellow at the University of Buckingham and shares his views @GoodwinMJ.

PREFACE

There are moments in the life of a nation when everything changes – not with a bang, not even with a conscious decision, but with a quiet, creeping loss of confidence so profound that a people start to forget who they are.

Britain, I believe, is living through such a moment. For decades, the institutions that once embodied our nation – Parliament, the civil service, the courts, the police, the BBC, the universities, the schools, the museums – have drifted away from the public they exist to serve. They no longer protect our interests; they merely perform a morality play for one another.

Our country is now in the grip of a new ruling class whose members see themselves not as custodians of a living nation, but as supervisors of a global humanitarian project that has no borders, no limits and no loyalty to the people whose taxes fund their salaries.

Their defining ideology, as I will show you, is 'suicidal empathy' – a deeply twisted worldview that is destroying our country in the name of showing empathy to others.

It is the belief that moral worth is measured not by defending your country but by demonstrating infinite generosity to the world, regardless of the consequences for your own nation and people.

The result is what you see around you today. A government without control. Borders without meaning. Public services without capacity. Leaders without courage. A country without confidence.

Britain is not falling because it is being pushed from the outside. It is falling because those on the inside – our own leaders – have lost the will to defend and conserve it.

This book is the story of how it happened: how a ruling elite in Westminster abandoned the public, how the public were never asked and how an entire nation has been reshaped in the name of a morality that punishes loyalty, pathologises belonging and treats national continuity as an embarrassment.

If we are to save our country, we must first understand how we lost it. I wrote this book as a contribution to this process.

Matt Goodwin
London, December 2025

INTRODUCTION

'Civilisations', wrote the historian and philosopher Arnold J. Toynbee, 'die from suicide, not by murder'. This book is the story of how Britain – or, rather, the people who run Britain – turned against their own nation. They are committing national suicide. This claim will strike many as controversial, even incendiary. But if you look with clear eyes at what is now unfolding at blistering speed it is the only logical conclusion that is left.

Within just one generation, Britain will no longer be Britain. England will no longer be England. The country that we still just about know and recognise, the country our ancestors built, will be no more. It will be replaced by something else.

Britain is not being conquered. It is not being invaded. Worse: it is being abandoned by the very people who were meant to protect it. It is not being pushed off a cliff. It is walking off one, led by a new generation of rulers who have clearly decided that maintaining the nation that was entrusted to them is no longer a priority.

For decades, these rulers have insisted that everything is fine – that the historic changes that are reshaping our towns, our cities, our schools, our culture and our very sense of home are 'normal', 'inevitable', or 'nothing to worry about'.

Yet millions of people in this country feel very differently. They share a single, heavy, unspoken, and at times overwhelming feeling. This feeling is not about a particular politician, a particular party, a particular government, or a particular policy.

It runs far deeper than that.

It is a feeling that most people try to suppress. They try to ignore it. They try to downplay it. Many simply find it too demoralising to confront.

Yet at the same time, deep down, in the pit of our stomach, we also know we cannot avoid it because it concerns the most treasured thing of all – our home. It can be expressed, I think, in just five words: **we are losing our country**.

THE DISPOSSESSED

Across Britain – in cities, towns, villages and suburbs – many people are now experiencing the same private, unspoken sense of shock.

You walk down a street you once knew and no longer recognise it. You visit the place where you were born yet now feel like a stranger. You hear languages that are not your own. You see customs and cultures you do not share.

The country of your childhood – the country once described to you by your parents and grandparents – no longer lies before you. It only seems to exist in old films, documentaries, fading books and nostalgia reels on social media.

Suddenly, the country you search for, the country you yearn for, the country you thought you would carry with you all along, is nowhere to be seen. It is as if, without warning, it vanished before your eyes. You have not left your country and yet you cannot shake the feeling your country has left you. It is, at root, a feeling of dispossession: a deeply troubling feeling that something you love is being taken from you without consent.

The English philosopher Sir Roger Scruton once said that a nation is more than just a set of documents, or what you see on your passport. A nation is home – built by our ancestors, conserved for generations and bound by a shared identity, history, culture and way of life.

It is not a cheap two-star hotel in which the person who is living next door is a stranger who speaks a different language, has a different culture and does not know your history. It is a community that is filled with your relatives, ancestors and neighbours, who you know and trust, and whose graves, stories and memories lay around you. It is a place that you instinctively recognise even if you might struggle to put it into words.

But today, when many people look out at the country they no longer see the home they once knew. They see a country that is being replaced by something else entirely.

The front door has been left not merely ajar but wide open. The walls are no longer secure. Anybody can walk in, regardless of who they are, where they are from, or what they intend to do. Even when they hurt us, they are allowed to stay.

This is not a fringe anxiety. It is now a major feeling in modern Britain, shared by millions of people. In 2025, a survey by the pollsters More In Common found that nearly half of all British people feel 'like a stranger in my own country', rising to three-quarters among those who are planning to vote Reform.[1]

Even the country's Labour Prime Minister Keir Starmer openly admitted in 2025 that Britain risks becoming an 'island of strangers' before hurriedly disowning his own words. But millions will think he was right the first time.

The feeling I am describing is not confined to one race or class. People from all backgrounds – White, Black, Asian – tell me they feel this way. People who grew up in a country that felt stable, familiar and coherent but now feel that the sheer speed and scale of the demographic changes that are sweeping through Britain are utterly bewildering, beyond all comprehension.

It is not just changing the population; it is severing people's sense of continuity with the country they once recognised, with the past they once knew. Many people from minority backgrounds feel this profound sense of loss just as strongly as those from the majority.

And yet, whenever people try to articulate this feeling – this creeping sense of dispossession – they are shamed, silenced, or mocked by the very elites who are imposing these changes on them from above.

The politicians who are doing this to the country tell you that what you are feeling is illegitimate. They tell you it is wrong to feel this way. That you must ignore it. They want you to silence yourself. They use all the usual tactics, all the usual words, to try and close down discussion of what I am about to show you.

They want you to feel ashamed and embarrassed for asking questions that you are entirely justified in asking. What is happening to my country? What is happening to my people? What is unfolding around us? And why is it even happening at all?

These questions are now crucial and urgent yet our politicians, the people who are paid to represent you, would rather you not ask them at all. To be dispossessed of the country you love is bad enough; but to be criticised and castigated for having the audacity to notice that dispossession and lament it is truly insufferable.

THE TRUTH WE CANNOT SAY

The reason so many people feel this way is because they know something precious and unique is slipping away. What we are witnessing in Britain, what I will show you in this book, is not just a small adjustment, a temporary shift, or the gentle evolution of a nation.

It is something far more dramatic and potentially permanent. What we are witnessing is the deliberate and sustained transformation of the only majority the country has ever known – the White British people – and hence the transformation of the country itself.

Nations will not remain the same if the very people who shaped them, built them and embody them collapse into minority status. If the core of a nation rapidly declines or is fully replaced, then that nation ceases to be the same nation. It becomes something else. It no longer really exists as it once did.

That is not an opinion. It is one of the most basic insights in the study of nations. The world's leading scholars – Walker Connor, Anthony Smith, Eric Kaufmann – all agree: nations depend upon an ethnic and cultural core, a historic majority, a thread of continuity. Without that core, the story that binds a people together unravels.

Britain's rulers know this. And yet, this is what they have chosen to pursue. Without democratic consent from the people they claim to represent, they are undertaking the single largest re-engineering of the population in its entire history.

THE YEAR 2063

Demography, it is often said, is destiny. So now consider the destiny that awaits Britain and its people if the country does not change course.

Look at the key trends that come from our country's official census, which I have examined in detail through my research and for this book.[2] By the end of this century, by the year 2100, the share of the country's population that is White British will collapse from 73% today, to just 33.7%.

The share of people who are foreign-born or the immediate descendants of foreign-born parents will rocket from 19% to over 60%. Muslims will go from representing about one in every seventeen people in Britain to one in every four, or one in every three among the young. This will all happen within the lifetime of a child born today, in the next seventy-four years.

When that child is in their twenties, by the year 2050, the White British will no longer be a majority among the country's young people. When they are in their thirties, by the year 2063, the White British will no longer be a majority in the country.

The country's historic majority will officially become a minority. What remains of the White British will grow older and become politically irrelevant.

At the same time, other demographic trends will reinforce people's profound feelings of loss, confusion and dispossession. When that child has grown older and is in their fifties, by the 2070s, they will be living in a country in which a large majority – more than six in ten people – were either born overseas or are the direct descendants of people who were. Most people will only be able to trace their roots back one or two generations at most.

Then, by the year 2100, when that child is in their seventies – if Britain retains its current policy of large-scale immigration from outside Europe – Islam will be easily the most powerful religion in the country, followed by at least one-quarter of the country.

The hushed debates that we are already starting to have – segregated Muslim areas, blasphemy laws, the rise of Islamic sectarianism in politics, the Pakistani Muslim rape gangs, the spread of anti-Semitism and the capacity of Islam to integrate into the Western nations – will all seem quaint by comparison. The balance of power will fundamentally shift.

That child born today, in other words, will not only live to see the demographic replacement of the country's historic majority but the complete transformation of the population. All the things Sir Roger Scruton said make a home – a shared national identity, culture, collective memory and way of life – will fade from view.

A change that took millennia to form will be undone in less than one human lifespan. It will be an astonishing change, a demographic and cultural revolution like nothing our country has seen. Just seventy-four years: that is how long it will take to witness the most influential nation in history – which gave the world liberty, reason, science, the Industrial Revolution, the English language, Shakespeare – becoming something else entirely.

This revolution is already underway. The White British are already a minority in our three largest cities – London, Manchester and Birmingham – as well as Leicester, Luton, Slough and Watford. Soon, if it is not already true, they will slide into minority status in Blackburn, Bradford, Cambridge, Coventry, Crawley, Milton Keynes, Nottingham, Oxford, Peterborough, Reading, Sandwell and Wolverhampton. Then, in Hertsmere, Bedford, Bexley, Oldham, Preston, Pendle, Thurrock, Derby, Havering and Bromley, among many more.

Most people will just stand by and watch this happen. Others, finding it too unbearable, will leave the country, as many are already starting to do. The only response from the ruling class is to ignore these trends or celebrate them.

At first, you were told that to even suggest such a change was ridiculous, conspiratorial, out of all proportion to the modest changes that are supposedly occurring. Now, you are told that the only politically correct response is to celebrate it.

WHY IT MATTERS

There are good reasons why all people – White, Black, Asian – should feel deeply concerned about what is about to unfold. The ethnic and cultural core of a nation is what holds it in place, like an anchor. It is what gives people, whether White or not, a sense of shared identity, culture, history, values and way of life. But once this anchor gives way, once the waves become too strong and overwhelming, there is nothing to hold the nation in place.

These truths are obvious everywhere on earth, except in the minds of Britain's ruling class which now works overtime to safeguard the identities of every group except the majority.

Many minorities feel just as strongly attached to this core as everybody else; they feel a strong bond to the only demographic make-up of Britain they have ever known. They see the historic majority as an important symbol of the community to which they belong and the sense of familiarity they feel. It is why people from minority backgrounds also voice strong concern about the level of immigration in Britain, or why one in every three backed Brexit.

There is a reason why more diverse nations are also less trusting, more divided and fragmented: because they do not have this unifying core. Most nations around the world have a clear majority. Roughly 70% have one, while 80% have one that represents at least 40%.

What will happen, then, when the White British slump to not just 14% of Newham, 20% of Harrow, or 28% of Westminster, as they are today, but just 33% of the entire *country*, as they are forecast to do by the end of the century?

Because of the trends that have been unleashed, which I will take you through in the next chapter, Britain is already on track to witness the rapid decline of its historic majority group, becoming one of the rare outliers in the world. Increasingly, if these trends continue, it will look more like Sierra Leone and Lebanon than the stable country we once knew, with politics becoming far more fractious, tribal and polarised, and civil unrest going mainstream.

This is not simply about race; it is about responsibility. When the delicate balance between newcomers and a country's historic population collapses, when the scale and speed of demographic change is so great, it is not only the majority who suffer.

Trust, cohesion and stability break down for everybody. The unspoken social contract between the people and their leaders, which relies upon people feeling respected and recognised, is torn apart. What follows is instability, division, chaos, even civil unrest.

You can already see the warning signs. The eruption of anti-Semitic protests in London, our capital city. The rise of 'homegrown' Islamist terrorists. State institutions such as West Midlands Police, in 2026, appearing to prioritise Islamist thugs when telling travelling Jewish football fans from Israel they are no longer welcome in Birmingham, the country's second city.

Look, too, at what the people themselves feel. In December 2025, the pollsters Ipsos-MORI found that nearly three-quarters of all British people – 74% – expect 'large-scale public unrest' to protest against the way the country is currently being governed.

Or look at the official data I will share with you in this book, such as the fact that there are now many people living among us who do not speak our language, do not share our identity and do not respect our way of life.

Ignoring this reality, pretending it does not exist, will only provoke an enormous backlash among people who might otherwise be open to accepting small amounts of immigration but who now worry, with good reason, what these seismic shifts, along with a culture of silence in Westminster, mean for their group, their culture and their country.

Change on this scale also risks blowing apart democracy. Nobody ever voted for Britain to be transformed in this way. Nobody was ever asked if they wanted it. And yet, still, this project proceeds, imposed from above without any consent.

THE QUESTION THEY WILL NOT ASK

There is one question that terrifies the ruling class: how did this happen?

How did a stable, coherent, deeply rooted nation – one with a millennia-old story – end up on a path that leads to its own dissolution?

The ruling class would like you to think this is the result of 'global forces', 'economic needs', 'natural change', or 'inevitable demographic trends'. But they are lying.

What has driven Britain to this point is not accident or fate, but ideology. As I will show you, the country is in the grip of a new ruling class – politicians, civil servants, academics, broadcasters,

NGOs, corporate executives, judges, activists, and more – that is guided by an entirely new moral code.

It is a deeply warped worldview which tells them that protecting and conserving a nation is shameful, that enforcing borders is cruel and unjust, that prioritising the very people who built the country is somehow immoral, that surrender is virtue while defence is sin, and that insiders must now come last because outsiders must come first.

It is an ideology that elevates compassion over continuity, sentiment over survival, performative empathy over duty; a belief system so warped that it leads a ruling class to dismantle and destroy the very country they are supposed to defend.

This ideology has been given a name, notably by the Canadian psychologist Gad Saad. It is *suicidal empathy*. It is the belief that extending limitless sympathy to outsiders is the highest form of goodness, even when doing so harms your own people.

It is what leads our rulers to open the borders while ignoring the consequences. It is what leads officials to ignore horrific scandals like the Pakistani Muslim rape gangs rather than be called 'racist'. It is what leads politicians to think it is reasonable to replace British workers with cheap imported labour from abroad. It is what leads governments to prioritise immigrants over their own citizens in housing, welfare and policing, while forcing their own citizens to pay for this warped social contract. It is what leads elites to treat their own people as a problem to be managed rather than a community to be protected. And it is what leads them to treat any defence of Britain as a moral failing and every act of surrender as a sign of virtue.

A country governed by this worldview will not survive, because suicidal empathy dismantles every instinct that is required for self-preservation.

This is not a conspiracy. There is no shadowy cabal. It is not the World Economic Forum, the United Nations, or the Fabians. Just a new ruling class in Westminster intoxicated by a distorted moral code – and willing to sacrifice our national continuity to uphold it.

WHAT I WILL SHOW YOU

In the pages ahead I shall walk you through what is happening to the country, why it is happening and what we can do to stop it before it is too late.

I will take you through all the key trends, data and evidence the ruling class would rather you not know, and which it works so tirelessly to conceal. They would rather you not read this book at all. It is ironic: the same people who accuse the people of 'misinformation' would rather they not have this information.

In the next chapter I will show you how the process of demographic replacement is already underway and accelerating. We will then explore what lies behind this, how a new ideology took control of the ruling class. Then, we turn to examine how this ruling class imposed an extreme policy of mass immigration without any democratic consent whatsoever. We then look at how illegal immigration and porous borders are compounding this process.

Next, we will examine how our taxpayer-funded institutions are contributing to this by imposing 'two-tier multiculturalism' on the country, a policy that works to preserve the identities of every group while working against the majority.

We look at how this deeply twisted worldview of suicidal empathy fuelled the biggest scandal in British history – the Pakistani Muslim rape gangs – and how the people who created it seek to silence anyone who dissents. Then, we turn to explore our capital city, London, where all the problems I describe in this book combine in one place.

Ultimately, we will see how Britain and its people now face a civilisational choice, one we can no longer avoid. The choice is ours: we can either choose to remain a country that we still just about know, recognise and find familiar, or we can allow our home to be fully replaced by something entirely different.

I did not write this book for the ruling class, for my former colleagues in the universities. It is not for the BBC or the media commentators who sneer at the people who pay their salaries and refuse to accept their concerns are legitimate.

I wrote it for the forgotten majority, for millions of people who work hard, pay taxes, obey the law and ask only to keep the country, the home, they inherited from their ancestors.

The elites will attack me because I wrote this for you. They will call me every name under the sun because I dare to tell you the truth. To sound the alarm. To tell you what is going on. To suggest an alternative way forward.

I did this because I genuinely believe that we might soon lose our final opportunity to remain in a stable, culturally coherent nation. As I wrote on social media, perhaps we have only two general elections left to push the country toward a different future from the one that awaits us. To which Elon Musk replied: 'No – you have one.'

It is hard to disagree. There are still unwritten chapters in our national story, but they will not write themselves. 'The British', it was once said, 'lose every battle – except the last'. That is how it now feels to millions of people – that we are approaching a critical moment.

Whether Britain remains Britain, whether England remains England, will depend on whether the people who built our country stand their ground and push back against the elite, or whether they allow the changes that I document in this book to unfold.

In the next chapter we will begin our journey by exploring the quiet revolution that is unfolding around us, a demographic transformation so vast and so rapid that most people have not yet grasped what it means. But they can feel it.

CHAPTER ONE

THE QUIET REPLACEMENT

The feeling, shared by millions today, of watching your country disappear, of losing your home, of losing a sense of the familiar, will be denied and dismissed in Westminster.

Politicians will tell you what you are feeling is irrational, that you are 'misinformed', that you have fallen for 'conspiracy theories'. Worse, they will try to make you ashamed for caring in the first place. If you persist, they will insult you for caring at all, denouncing you as 'extreme', 'racist', or 'far right'.

But this common feeling – that we are losing something precious, something unique – is not irrational. It is the only sane response to what is unfolding. The transformation of our country, including the demographic replacement of the historic majority, is no longer hidden from view. It is now a fact.

For years, even to mention the word 'replacement' was to invite excommunication from polite society. It was cast as a dark fantasy, an unforgivable idea. Even to discuss it was considered taboo; to suggest such a process might be encouraged or tolerated by the people whose duty is to safeguard the country was considered beyond the pale.

But what was once cast as fringe or conspiratorial is now undeniable. Whatever you think of the motives behind it, the reality can be counted, mapped and described.

Official statistics tell the story clearly. No one can seriously pretend we are still in the realm of conspiracy theory, especially after they reach the end of this chapter.

If you want to know where a nation is going, look at where it has just been. In this chapter I will show you the sheer speed and scale of the trends that are rapidly redefining the country. They not only reveal how fast the majority is being displaced; they also show how profound these changes will be for the next generation.

We can see how radical this transformation is by comparing the census for England and Wales in 2001 with the one twenty years later, in 2021. In only two decades, the country has already been remade. What is coming over the next seventy-four years will be the rapid acceleration of trends that are already underway.

In this chapter, the story comes in three parts. The first is the rapid decline of the White British. The second is the explosive rise of the foreign-born. The third is why this matters – how these shifts are eroding the deeper foundations that hold our country together.

THE VANISHING MAJORITY

Let's start with the decline of the White British. For much of our recent history, the White British – the country's historic core – comprised more than nine in ten people.

But in just twenty years after 2001, their share collapsed by thirteen points, falling below three-quarters. Over the same period, the share of people who are *not* White British more than doubled, to 26% – more than one in four people.

Between the eras of Tony Blair and Boris Johnson, the number of non-Whites in the country surged from 6.5 million to some 15.2 million.

Because of these shifts, as I noted in the Introduction, the White British, who made up roughly 95% of the country as

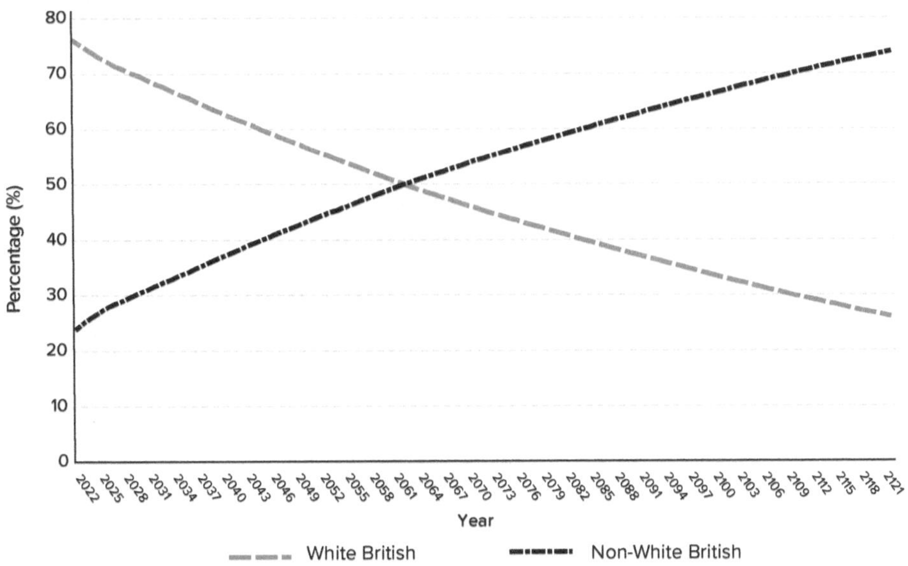

Percentage of the population identifying as White British, United Kingdom, 2022–2121

recently as the 1990s, are on course to become a minority by the year 2063.

We can already see this in our largest cities – Birmingham, London, and Manchester – where the White British are *already* a minority, as well as in Leicester, Slough and Watford.

These trends are now cascading into surrounding areas so that what is already visible in the big cities will soon become visible on their outskirts, then in large towns, then smaller towns, then villages.

Already today the White British are a minority in about 1,200 neighbourhoods (or in census-speak 'middle super output areas'). This figure will only surge in the years ahead as they inch closer to minority status across Britain. In some neighbourhoods the majority is not just a minority; it has nearly disappeared, making up fewer than one in ten people.

If you want to see what this looks like on the ground, go to St Matthew's in Leicester, in the East Midlands, which is known locally as 'Mashtown', 'Hell City', or 'Little Somalia'. Here, amid the countless Turkish barbershops, mosques and Somali stores, only 3% of local people are White British, nearly 70% are Asian and almost three-quarters are Muslim.

Leicester matters because for years the ruling class held it up as a success story, a place where 'diversity works'. If you want to be reassured about the transformation of Britain, they said, look at Leicester. Everything there is fine.

But official statistics tell a very different story. In this part of the city, not even one in three households speak English as their main language while nearly one in three residents refuse to share a British or English identity, preferring to align themselves with what the country's census calls a 'non-UK identity' instead.

In 2022, interethnic tension between local Hindus and Muslims after a cricket match quickly spiralled into mass unrest on the streets, complete with chants and violent clashes over much broader geopolitical issues in faraway lands.

Two years later, local Muslims in Leicester also rejected mainstream British politics by electing a 'pro-Gaza' independent Muslim MP, showing how in areas like this, once held up as the future of Britain, religious and tribal allegiances are rapidly displacing national ones.

For years, Leicester was sold to us as the model for managing diversity. But today, no serious person would say it is a success. Leicester is not an outlier; it is a warning. At the 2021 census, it became one of the first cities in the country where the White British are a minority.

In the next few years, this will be the case in many other places. From Blackburn to Bradford, Cambridge to Coventry, Nottingham to Reading, Peterborough to Sandwell, Oxford to Wolverhampton, the White British will slide into minority status, if they have not already done so by the time you read this. Slightly later, the same will happen in Crawley, Milton Keynes, Hertsmere, Bedford, Bexley, Oldham, Preston, Pendle, Thurrock, Derby, Bromley, Welwyn, Hatfield, Woking, Dartford and Walsall, and many more places.

If you want to see another possible future that awaits Britain, visit the borough of Blackburn with Darwen, in Lancashire, where only a little over half of residents are White British and their share has collapsed by ten points in just ten years.

In many parts of the town, terrace houses that were once filled with White British families are now almost entirely occupied by families of Pakistani or Indian heritage.

In 2001, the academic Ted Cantle's report on northern towns like these shattered the cosy myth of multicultural harmony. Courageously, Cantle warned that White British and Muslim communities were already living 'parallel lives', with little mixing.

Twenty years later, for his book *Among the Mosques: A Journey Across Muslim Britain*, published in 2021, Ed Husain visited many of the same areas and reported that some young Muslims in Britain can go an entire day – from attending their local school to mosque – without having any meaningful interactions with people from the non-Muslim majority.

Both Cantle and Husain were attacked by the politically correct ruling class in London, Oxford and Cambridge. But the demographic results speak for themselves.

In Blackburn with Darwen, there are neighbourhoods where fewer than 2% of people are White British, while more than 90% are Muslims of Pakistani or Indian heritage. In neighbourhoods like Bastwell, in Blackburn, only about half of all households speak English as their main language, and in some parts close to one in three people openly say they do not identify with the United Kingdom, Britain, or England. Does any of this look like a success story? Do people want the rest of Britain to look like Leicester or Blackburn with Darwen?

Or look at the town of Luton, in Bedfordshire, where the White British share has collapsed from 65% in 2001 to just 31% today. Luton, too, is no model for the future. It is well known for having incubated Islamist extremism and high levels of segregation.

White British people who remain in Luton are now largely confined to outer areas while many neighbourhoods are highly segregated by ethnicity and religion. In some parts of Luton only a small minority of households speak English as their main language and close to half of all residents refuse to share our national identity.

We could walk through the same patterns in many parts of Birmingham, Bradford, Manchester, Oldham, and large parts of London – places where the White British are now most noticeable by their absence, and where the shared foundations of our national life, including a shared language and a shared sense of identity, are crumbling.

Do you want the rest of Britain to look like Leicester, Blackburn and Luton? Because this is the direction in which the current trends are pointing.

TOMORROW IS ALREADY HERE

If you want to see the future of a country, do not only look at its recent past. Look at its children. Nothing reveals the sheer scale and speed of Britain's transformation more honestly than what is happening in the country's schools and nurseries.

Consider the school register. Once, names like Thomas, Jack, Oliver and Noah dominated the list. By 2023, Muhammad – in the top ten since 2016 – had officially replaced Noah as the most popular boy's name in the country. Interestingly, a new entry in 2024 was Yahya, the name of the Hamas leader who oversaw the worst mass murder of Jews since the Second World War.

These are not trivial curiosities. They reflect deeper currents that are sweeping through Britain's schools and will soon sweep through the entire country.

In 2001, the White British made up 83% of all children under four; by 2021, it was 66%. Two years later, in 2023, it was quietly reported that barely half of all babies born in Britain were White British, down from 65% a decade earlier.

This is not a slow, gentle shift. This is not a continuation of the past. Among the young, the demographic revolution has already happened. We are merely waiting for older people to pass away.

White British children are already a minority in one in four schools in the country, including almost all parts of London.

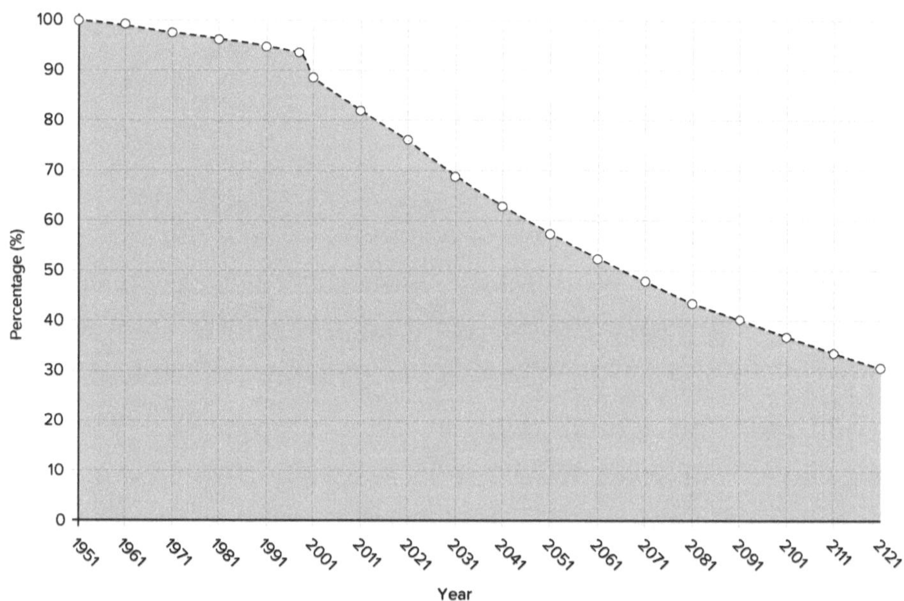

The decline of the White British majority, 1951–2121. White British Share (%)

Nearly four in ten schoolchildren now come from minority ethnic backgrounds, a ten-point surge in just ten years.[3]

In primary schools, White British children are already a minority in not just almost all of London but Blackburn, Bolton, Bradford, Manchester, Oldham, Derby, Coventry, Sandwell, Walsall, Bedford, Wolverhampton, Peterborough, Thurrock, Milton Keynes, Reading and Slough. They make up only 35% of primary pupils in Nottingham, 25% in Birmingham, 20% in Leicester, 13% in Luton, 10% in Slough, 8% in Tower Hamlets and 5% in Newham.

There are many schools where White British children are barely visible at all. In 2006, for instance, there were some 760 schools where they made up fewer than one in ten pupils. Today, that number has surged to 1,400. Astoundingly, there are nearly 500 schools where White British children make up less than 2% of pupils, and 72 schools where not a single White British child appears on the school register.[4]

The speed of change is staggering. It is scarcely believable. Take St Mary's Wavendon Church of England Primary School in Milton Keynes. There the share of White British pupils collapsed from 84% in 2006 to 32% by 2022. At St Joseph's Catholic Primary School in Oxford, it collapsed from 74 to 19%. At St John's in Stoke-on-Trent, from 89% to 40%.[5]

This is not evolution; this is displacement.

In state nurseries, the trends are even more striking. White British toddlers now make up only 19% of nursery pupils in Manchester, 16% in Nottingham, 14% in Luton, 13% in Bradford, 12% in Kirklees, 8% in Coventry and just 5% in Slough.

What this shows is how the transformation is being driven by age. The average White British person is forty-five years old, compared to twenty-seven for Bangladeshis, twenty-eight for Pakistanis and Arab, thirty for Black Africans, thirty-two for those recorded as Black and thirty-six for Indians. You do not need to be a demographer to see where this leads.

The White British will rapidly shrink – becoming less visible, less influential, less powerful – while a more diverse and fragmented population grows in its place. In plain English, the country will lose its distinctiveness, its collective memory, its story and its continuity with the past. This brings us to the second part of the story: the foreign-born tide.

THE FOREIGN-BORN TIDE

Between 2001 and 2021, the share of foreign-born residents in Britain, people who were not born in the country, soared to 17%. Today, thanks in large part to the changes that were made under Boris Johnson and the Tories, which I shall examine in Chapter 3, it is closer to 20%.

In other words, nearly one in five people who are currently living in Britain – roughly 13 million – were not born in this country. While many of these people will feel British and passionately support the country, by definition it is also true they cannot have the same instinctive, emotional connection to our identity, history and landscape as those whose families have been here for generations.

Politicians try to distract you from this reality, by repeating the same line: Britain, they say, has 'always been a nation of immigrants'. But this is false. Between the 1800s and 1921, the share of foreign-born never exceeded 2.5% and was usually closer to 1.5%.

From 1951, the share of foreign-born people edged upwards, but remained below 8% until 2001. So, no, Britain was not 'built by immigrants'.

As political commentator and author Konstantin Kisin, himself born in Russia, has pointed out, while immigrants have played 'a small but not insignificant role' in our history, 'Britain's glory days were built by its native population'.

From 2001, however, everything changed. The foreign-born population exploded.

Between 2011 and 2021, the UK-born population grew by just 2%, while the foreign-born population grew by 33%. By 2025, the

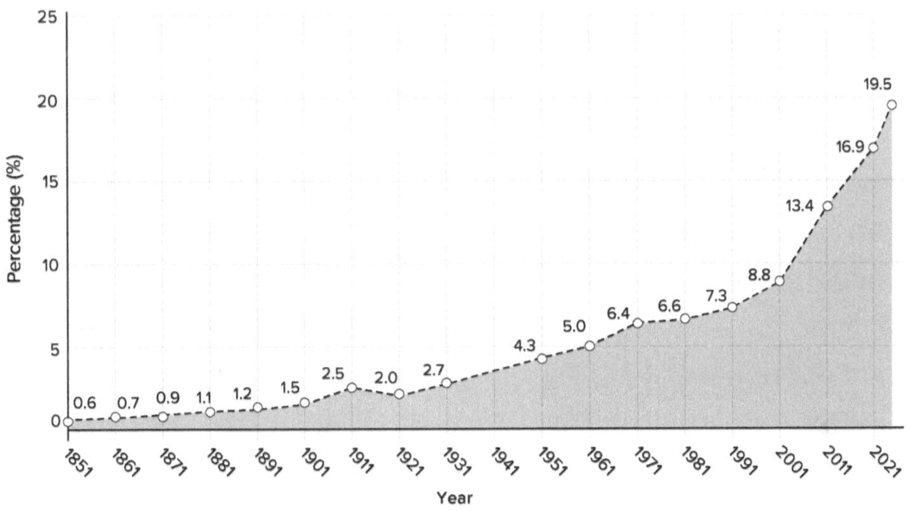

Foreign-born population of England and Wales, 1851–2025

foreign-born share in Britain was higher than it had been in the United States at the height of the Ellis Island era in the 1920s, a spike that prompted America to slam the breaks on mass immigration for the next forty years.

Births tell the same story. Since the late 1990s, the share of babies with two British-born parents has collapsed from nearly three-quarters to just 57%. Soon, children born to a mother and father who were themselves born in Britain, creating families with strong, multigenerational roots in the country, will be a minority.

The very latest data makes the point even more starkly. In 2025, it was revealed that more than 40% of *all* babies born in Britain had at least one foreign-born parent, and close to 30% had two foreign-born parents.[6]

In a wide belt across London – Brent, Newham, Harrow, Ealing, Westminster, the Square Mile – more than 80% of babies now have at least one foreign-born parent. The same pattern is emerging well beyond the capital: Luton (79%), Slough (78%), Leicester (71%), Oxford (68%), Watford and Manchester (65%), Birmingham (62%) and Nottingham (57%).

In places like Bradford, Derby, Milton Keynes, Reading, Sandwell, Southampton, Woking and Wolverhampton, more than half of all babies are now born to at least one foreign-born parent. Soon, this will be true in Bolton, Oldham, Salford, Hertsmere, Dartford, Gravesham, Ipswich, Preston, Bedford and Swindon.

Why does this matter, some will ask? It matters because when a fast-growing share of the population is only one or two generations removed from somewhere else, the shared memories, symbols and emotional bonds that once united that country will inevitably weaken – if they are not diluted beyond recognition.

Today, this is intensified by the fact that most foreign-born migrants are no longer coming from culturally similar nations in Europe or the wider Anglosphere. Far from it.

In 2024, the most common countries of origin for foreign-born mothers included India, Pakistan, Nigeria, Bangladesh, Ghana, Afghanistan and Iraq – all nations with radically different cultures, identities, religions and ways of life from our own.

Immigration is not only about the movement of people; it is also about the movement of cultures. By reshaping our population around the foreign-born, we are reshaping our country around cultures that are radically different from, and sometimes deeply at odds with, our own.

Ask yourself plainly: do you want the political, social and religious cultures of Pakistan, Nigeria, Bangladesh, Afghanistan, Albania and Iraq to be imported into Britain at scale? These are societies that are often marked by deep ethnic and religious divisions, low trust in institutions and completely different ideas about justice, family, sexuality, women's rights, the separation of church and state and the role of religion in public life.

This is not an abstract question. This is what is happening now, and it will have consequences for the kind of country our children inherit.

THE WIDER CRISIS

Many people will draw a straight line from these changes to immigration. But immigration is only one part of a wider demographic crisis that is now facing our country.

Astonishingly, while this crisis will have an enormous impact on the future of our country it is also one that very few people in Westminster are even willing to discuss.

The point is simple: the British have stopped having children. Our birth rate is collapsing. As population expert Dr Paul Morland puts it: 'Demography is destiny. Nations that cease to believe in themselves stop reproducing and nations that stop reproducing eventually cease to exist.' That is the only conclusion an honest person can draw.

Britain's fertility rate has been below replacement for more than half a century. We have not been reproducing ourselves since 1972. You will not hear much about this from Westminster or the BBC. If you try to talk about Britain's plunging birth rate – and the urgent need to have more children – the ruling class will look at you as though you are mad.

But the demographic crisis is unavoidable. It is basic arithmetic.

For a population to remain stable across generations, the fertility rate must be about 2.1 children per woman – the 'replacement rate'. But in 2025, it was quietly announced that the rate in England and Wales had fallen to a record low of just 1.41. In Scotland it was 1.25.

Nowhere near what is needed. And because women who were born outside Britain tend to have more children on average than those who were born in Britain, the fertility rate among the historic majority, the White British, is lower still. Yet no frontline politician is prepared to ask the most obvious question: how do we help British families have more children?

All over the world, from Hungary to South Korea, countries are debating this question openly. But in Britain, to merely raise it is to be treated as dangerous or eccentric. If anything, politicians seem determined to do the opposite of what is required.

In 2025, for instance, the Labour government removed the 'two-child cap' for welfare benefits, expanding state support for larger families, but without setting any clear criteria or priority for British families. The main beneficiaries, it was later revealed, will disproportionately be families of Pakistani, Bangladeshi, Nigerian and Somali heritage, all groups that are more likely to have three or more children.

A report by the Westminster think tank Policy Exchange found that while the share of families with three or more children is 14% among the White British, it is 38% in Bangladeshi families and 41% in Pakistani ones.

A freedom of information request submitted to the British state by Conservative Member of Parliament Nick Timothy revealed that nearly 350,000 foreign-born families will benefit from extra welfare handouts, with nearly 200,000 coming from only ten countries, including Pakistan, Bangladesh, Nigeria, Somalia, India, Ghana, Afghanistan and Iraq.

In other words, the same political class that presided over these destabilising trends is now forcing British taxpayers to subsidise a welfare policy that will disproportionately support foreign-born families.

If the British are no longer reproducing themselves, then why is the population still growing at unprecedented speed? Because our population growth is being driven almost entirely by what we will examine in Chapter 3: mass uncontrolled immigration.

Britain is no longer growing through what demographers call 'natural change' among the native-born – with the number of British births exceeding deaths. It is now only growing because of immigration, which is fast-tracking the demographic replacement of the majority.

If you want one statistic that captures this process it is this: by 2025, mass immigration accounted for 98% of *all* population growth in Britain, with the remaining 2% coming from births to the foreign-born. This has never happened before in history. It is unprecedented.

Our future will no longer be shaped by British people having children – by families with deep roots and long memories – but by the arrival and reproduction of new populations that often barely know the country at all.

Mass immigration was sold as a way to halt demographic decline and ensure there were young workers to support an ageing society. If that was the goal, it has failed. The British birth rate continues to fall. The decline of the White British majority accelerates. And mass immigration, as we will see, has made the country far more fragmented, divided and polarised.

Meanwhile, the same politicians who opened Britain's doors now refuse to talk about the collapsing birth-rate and disappearance of the majority. That silence is not an accident.

It is part of the project.

THE ERODING FOUNDATIONS

All the demographic changes that I describe are celebrated in London, Oxford and Cambridge. Elites insist they are an unqualified good, that they are 'strengthening' Britain.

But is this really true? For a nation to endure, it requires a minimum of three basic things: a shared language, a shared identity and a shared religion or values. Without these, a nation is not really a nation at all.

Look at the official data and you find that, under the sheer weight of these demographic trends, these foundations – long taken for granted – are now crumbling.

Take religion, specifically our Christian heritage that has long shaped who we are.

In 2021, it was revealed for the first time that Britain is no longer a majority-Christian nation. In just twenty years, from 2001 to 2021, the number of Christians in England and Wales fell by ten million, falling from 72% to just 46% of the population.

The British Social Attitudes survey tells the same story more starkly, with Christianity falling from two-thirds of the population as recently as the 1980s to about one-third today.

Weekly attendance at Church of England services has collapsed from 1.1 million to around 685,000, less than 1% of the country. Among eighteen-to-twenty-four-year-olds, only 1% identify as Anglican. Roughly 3,500 churches closed permanently in the decade to 2024.

It could be worse. At least the hate crimes against Christians and arson attacks on their churches that are recorded elsewhere in the world have not yet become a feature here. Yet.

As Christianity retreats, two groups have surged: the non-religious and Muslims.

Between 2001 and 2021, the share of people with 'no religion' more than doubled to nearly 40%. Over the same period, the number of Muslims doubled to nearly four million. Islam, not Christianity, is now the fastest growing religion in Britain.

Compare their rate of growth. In the decade leading up to the last census, in 2021, the Christian population declined by 17% while the Muslim population grew by 43%. In a single decade, Muslims, who are also significantly younger than Christians, went from representing one in every twenty people to one in every fifteen.

By the end of the present century, they are projected to be roughly one in every four adults and one in every three young people. Muslims already comprise 40% of Tower Hamlets, a third of Blackburn, Bradford and Newham, 30% of Birmingham and Slough, and a quarter of places like Pendle, Oldham, Leicester, Barking and Dagenham and Manchester.

Elites tell us this is not a problem because British Muslims are integrating into the nation. But in many parts of Britain – Birmingham, Blackburn, Bolton, Bradford, Derby, Kirklees, Luton,

Leicester, Manchester, Oldham, Pendle, Sandwell, Sheffield and Walsall – there are already highly segregated Muslim enclaves with little interaction across group lines.

Under the pressure of large-scale immigration and the absence of assimilation, entire communities have become ghettoised. And if you dare point this out, you are 'Islamophobic'.

Islam will not only grow in numbers; it will also grow in political influence. The harassment and intimidation that many Labour MPs experienced from pro-Gaza activists in heavily Muslim areas during the 2024 general election campaign was just the start.

Muslims are already the largest religious group in nearly twenty Westminster seats. In 2024, they were the largest minority religion in nearly 60% of all marginal seats. Soon, they will completely dominate politics in large parts of Birmingham, Blackburn, Bradford, Kirklees, Manchester and Oldham, as they already do in parts of London.

Global trends point in the same direction. Between 2010 and 2020, the Pew Research Center noted that Muslims worldwide are growing at more than twice the rate of non-Muslims. By 2050, if Europe continues its current policy of large-scale immigration, the Muslim share of the population is projected to reach 31% in Sweden, 20% in Germany, 18% in France and Belgium and 17% in Britain.[7] These are not wild speculations; they are demographic projections based on current trends. They will pose profound challenges for Western nations.

Yet in Westminster nobody seriously wants to talk about them, least of all the politicians who have overseen them.

A SHARED LANGUAGE?

If a shared religion is fading, then a shared language is also fragmenting.

Most people around the world think that speaking a shared national language is important to their national identity. In 2024, the independent Pew Research Center found that nearly 90 per cent of people in Britain think this way.[8] But what happens when millions no longer speak the national tongue?

This is not a question our ancestors really had to think about; but it is one we can no longer ignore. Between 2011 and 2021, the number of people in England and Wales whose main language is not English shot past 5.1 million.

Think about that for a moment. More than five million people in the country now prefer to speak a language other than English. While the population of English speakers grew by about 5% over this period, the number of people who prefer another language grew nearly five times faster, by 23%.

The ruling class and their cheerleaders – Keir Starmer, Sadiq Khan, Tony Blair, Emily Maitlis, Alastair Campbell, James O'Brien and the rest – will tell you that 'diversity is our strength' and 'immigration makes Britain stronger'. But what they will not dwell on is the fact, shared by the UK Statistics Authority, that nearly one million people in England cannot speak English well or at all. Meanwhile, only just over half of migrants aged over sixteen say English is their main language and only 38% say they can speak it well.

These figures also hide considerable variation. According to a report published in late 2025 by the Migration Advisory Committee, which advises the government, roughly one in three women who migrated to Britain from Afghanistan, Bangladesh, Turkey and Syria cannot speak English well or at all, alongside one in four Pakistani women.

If you want a glimpse of the country's future, then visit places like Newham, Brent, Ealing, Harrow, Leicester, Slough, Tower Hamlets or Westminster, where more than one in four residents no longer speak English as their main language.

In Enfield, Luton, Barnet, Camden, Boston and Cambridge, more than one in five do not speak English as their primary language. Soon, Peterborough, Watford, Reading, Coventry, Nottingham and Southampton will likely join them.

The erosion of a shared language is also further weakening our country. The Migration Advisory Committee finds that migrants who do not speak English are less likely to be in work, less likely to earn as much as other people and less engaged in community life, such as taking part in politics or volunteering. It also imposes enormous costs on the British people.

In 2025, the health service reported that one in ten patients do not have 'functional English language skills', with most instead speaking Urdu or Bengali. Translation services in the NHS have more than doubled in just five years.

Such is the state of affairs that in 2021 officials who run the country's census had to provide translation leaflets in more than fifty languages – the most common being Polish, Romanian, Panjabi, Urdu, Arabic, Bengali and Gujarati.

The Department for Work and Pensions now spends around £6 million a year on translation. Why? Because more than 1.2

million foreigners now claim Universal Credit welfare benefits, at a cost of around £10 *billion* a year. In 2025, the NHS spent £64 million solely on translation services, enough to cover the annual salaries of nearly 2,000 nurses.

The costs, as always, fall on British taxpayers who never voted for these demographic changes in the first place.

The picture is even more alarming in schools, the institutions that will shape our future. Between 1997 and 2023, the share of school pupils who speak 'English as an Additional Language', because they speak a different language at home, nearly tripled to more than 20%. More than 1.7 million pupils now speak English as an additional language.

Nearly one in four primary school children – and close to one in three nursery children – no longer speak English as their main language.[9] Shockingly, in recent years fawning BBC articles pointed to the fact that in at least one primary school in Bradford, for example Feversham Primary Academy, 'more than 98 per cent of pupils speak English as an additional language, the vast majority being from a Pakistani background'.[10] I find this deeply alarming. Don't you?

It is now not uncommon in Britain to find schools where dozens of different languages are spoken, which introduces huge challenges for teachers. In 2023, the Bell Foundation submitted evidence to Parliament and noted 'teaching and support staff are less confident working in multilingual classrooms'. Only a little more than one-third of new teachers said they felt prepared for teaching in multilingual classrooms, while in 2026 one newspaper revealed British taxpayers now have to pay £572 million to cater for pupils who have English as an additional language.[11] And what, we might ask, about the impact of all this on native English-speaking children, who – unlike their predecessors – suddenly have to navigate classrooms that may be filled with pupils from around the world, speaking different languages, clinging to different cultures and with whom they may have vanishingly little in common? Are we not allowed to consider them?

This is not multicultural harmony or enrichment. It is the dismantling of the shared linguistic foundations on which a functioning education system depends. It is what demographic upheaval looks like on the ground: schools where a shared language that once united communities has collapsed in a single generation.

Take Newcastle, for example. In some areas of this city one in three children no longer use English as their main language. Similar or more extreme patterns can be found in Bury (42%), Birmingham (45%), Manchester (48%), Kent (51%), Kirklees (55%), Nottingham (57%), Cheshire East (67%), Coventry (72%) and Harrow (86%).

In Leicester, Luton, Slough and virtually all of London, most primary school pupils' main language is no longer English. In places like Derby, Bolton, Oldham, Coventry, Sandwell, Milton Keynes and Reading between a third and a half of *all* primary pupils no longer speak English as their preferred language. In two primary schools – one in Tower Hamlets, one in West Yorkshire – not a single child speaks English as their native tongue.

This is, put simply, not sustainable.

WHO ARE WE?

If shared language is the glue, then a shared national identity is the anchor.

In his influential book *Who Are We? The Challenges to America's National Identity*, published in 2004, the scholar Samuel P. Huntington argued that a shared identity is absolutely essential for a nation's survival.

But here, too, the warning lights are flashing red. Between 2011 and 2021, the number of people in Britain who say they do not identify with a British, English, or UK identity surged to nearly six million, close to 10% of the population.

In much of London, between a quarter and a third of residents openly refuse to embrace any of our national identities. In Boston, Coventry, Leicester, Luton, Manchester, Peterborough and Reading, about one in five people do the same, preferring to align themselves with a 'non-UK identity'.

Ask yourself a question nobody in power will raise: how can you build a prosperous, cohesive and stable nation when millions of people in that nation neither speak the national language nor share its national identity?

Among Muslims, one of the fastest growing groups, the picture is sharper still. While it is true that some surveys suggest Muslims feel a strong sense of belonging to the country, other recent studies also point in a far more worrying direction.

In 2025, for instance, a major survey by research consultancy Whitestone Insight asked Muslims in Britain whether they identify 'first and foremost' with Islam or with a British, English or

Scottish identity. The result was decisive and was not close: 71% said they identify first and foremost with Islam, while only 27% first with a national identity.

This is what happens when people no longer have a shared sense of collective memory, national identity and emotional loyalty to the nation; they either prioritise a narcissistic individualism, thinking only of themselves, or they break off into competing identity groups. Once the foundations of a nation state give way, people hunker down in smaller tribes or retreat into private individualism. Either path weakens the shared sense of 'we' that a nation needs if it is to endure over the longer term.

That, increasingly, is where Britain now finds itself.

A QUESTION OF SURVIVAL

The ruling class will not dwell on any of this. They will dismiss it as paranoia, exaggeration, or scaremongering. But the numbers reveal the truth.

The country's historic majority is being demographically replaced and, within a few decades, will fall into minority status. This demographic replacement will not simply change Britain; it will change what the country *is*.

We can already see the foundations of our shared life – religion, language, identity – eroding under the pressure of these changes. As the ethnic and cultural core breaks down and is replaced, so too will the nation that grew out of it.

Do we wish to survive as a nation? History offers no guaranteed places. Peoples come and go. Many – the Phoenicians, the Carthaginians, the Jutes – have all vanished into dust.

What must the British and English do if they want to avoid the same fate? At a minimum, as we can see reflected in the numbers I have shared in this chapter, they must reverse the collapse in births, defend their culture and reassert their language and identity.

Above all, though, they must defend themselves from what we will examine in the next chapter: a ruling class that turned against its own country and people by opening the gates, dismissing those who noticed and undermining the nation from within.

CHAPTER TWO

SUICIDAL EMPATHY

How did Britain arrive at this point? What made the sheer speed and scale of the demographic changes that we have just examined possible?

Many on the right of politics will say that the transformation of the country is happening through an external invasion. But this is wrong: it is taking place through surrender.

Let me be clear about one point. Our country, our home, is not being weakened by the people arriving on our shores in ever larger numbers; it is being dismantled by the politicians who opened the gates without consent or care, and who now refuse to close them.

The people who claim to represent us have either decided to end the life of the country as we have known it or no longer have any serious interest in stopping this from happening. Increasingly, they neither represent, nor even seem to like, the people who put them into office.

Whether on the left or the right, whether Labour or Tory, politicians have surrendered to the forces that are now transforming the country at speed – or, even worse, are actively encouraging them.

It is easy to focus on headline issues like soaring legal immigration or the spiralling number of illegal migrants crossing the Channel in small boats. But these are symptoms, not the disease.

The huge shifts you saw in the previous chapters did not fall from the sky; they are the product of a much deeper moral and institutional sickness that has taken hold of our country.

The real cause of our national unravelling is not immigrants or refugees. It is a new ruling class that longer believes in the nation, no longer values its historic majority and no longer really cares about the continuity of the country and its people.

Majorities are only replaced when elites cease to believe they have a special claim on the land, culture, or future of their own home. That is precisely what is happening. A new ruling class has, like an aggressive cancer, taken hold, metastasising wherever power is held. It is using that power to remake Britain around a deeply deranged worldview: suicidal empathy.

Before we go any further, let me define this phrase. Suicidal empathy is a one-way, unconditional compassion that always favours outsiders over your own people, even when it damages your nation, undermines your safety and threatens your survival.

It is what happens when leaders turn admirable instincts – compassion and empathy – into self-destructive beliefs that destroy a nation from within. When politicians demand limitless sympathy for outsiders regardless of behaviours or consequence, while treating the majority as suspicious, outdated, irrelevant, or expendable.

It is an impulse that insists a nation must always favour whoever appears weaker or marginalised, even if doing so dismantles a country from within. It brands any attempt by the majority to defend their own interests – even their very survival – as bigotry or hatred.

In this chapter I will explain who these people are and how this deadly new virus among the ruling class has taken hold. In the chapters that follow, I will then show how this creed is translated into concrete policies that are transforming the nation and setting the stage for the demographic replacement of the majority: mass immigration, open borders, 'two-tier' multiculturalism and the suppression of dissent.

FROM OLD ELITE TO NEW ELITE

Britain was not always ruled by the kind of elites you see around you today.

As I showed in my previous book, *Values, Voice and Virtue*, published in 2023, the country was once governed by an Old Elite that would never have allowed the profound shifts that we explored in previous chapters to take place.[12] It was comprised of aristocrats, politicians, clergy and intellectuals, many of whom were shaped by the experience of two world wars.

They lived privileged lives, but they were openly patriotic and keenly aware of their sense of duty and obligation to the nation. They believed deeply in the nation's inheritance – its culture, institutions, and continuity – and saw themselves as its guardians.

They felt what Edmund Burke called 'reverence' – the idea that we should treat the country as something sacred, a trust handed down from one generation to the next, not something to be casually destroyed or torn up on a whim.

How distant this seems today. Unlike then, today's New Elite deny, sneer at, or rewrite the past while shutting their eyes to the degraded future they are creating.

They proclaim they are 'on the right side of history', which usually means winning approval from their peers today, not preserving the country so it can be passed on to future generations. Their loyalties lie not with Britain but with a global class of other elites.

Their agenda is only designed to impress one another, not safeguard the nation. As Keir Starmer openly admitted in 2023, he prefers Davos to Westminster. Starmer was merely saying out loud what the members of this New Elite secretly believe – a confession of allegiance to the global managerial class, the belief that all power should be invested in elites, not the people.

They also ignore the ancient warning of Cicero, the Roman statesman, who once wrote in Latin '*Salus populi suprema lex esto*', which means 'the good of the people should be the supreme law of the land'. When leaders abandon that sacred duty to their own people, they weaken the state from within, leaving it vulnerable to external invasions and, eventually, collapse. This is what is happening in Britain today.

THE GUIDING CREED

Today's ruling class has been shaped by a philosophy that treats nations as morally suspect and borders as artificial. It has little time at all for the idea of nation-states and national citizens, never mind the need to put people from your own country first.

It is the creed of universal liberalism, which tells elites that their first duty is not to their own people but to 'humanity' in general. Taken in moderation, showing compassion to others is admirable. But taken to excess, as I will show you, it becomes suicidal.

I am not the first person to point to how today's elites have drifted away from everybody else. Many writers have already shown this.

James Burnham exposed the rise of a remote managerial class in the West, that feels little loyalty to ordinary people; Christopher Lasch warned that elites were becoming 'tourists in their own nations', no longer capable of forging attachments to place; Sir Roger Scruton lamented the loss of a shared sense of loyalty and obligation among leaders and warned they were turning against their own nation; David Goodhart showed how nations have been hijacked by the 'Anywheres' – a highly mobile, left-leaning, elite graduate class that values achieved identities – who have taken control from the 'Somewheres' who feel strongly rooted in, and value, their ascribed identities, including the nation.

What they have all shown is how an old, nationally minded, civic elite has been replaced by a new, global, post-national, technocratic elite that feels little loyalty to the nation, has no real accountability to the people, and no serious interest in representing or respecting them.

Global in outlook and tastes, the New Elite instinctively favour international institutions over national democracy, international elites over national citizens. They see the rest of society, the people, as not only hopelessly provincial but morally inferior.

They have largely lost the capacity for local and national attachments. If they talk about national identity then it is only ever discussed in terms of how it can be hollowed out and reshaped on global lines.

The only debate about British or English identity that excites the New Elite is the prospect of remaking these national identities into global, rootless ones. Seen through their eyes, there is nothing distinctive or unique about these identities; they are merely vessels through which we celebrate global 'diversity'.

This is reflected in the language they use. Whereas the Old Elite spoke of virtue, honour, duty, service and patriotism, the New Elite talk endlessly and obsessively about diversity, equality, inclusion, tolerance, empathy and fairness. It is a language that is not interested in the nation at all. Their obsession with diversity is never truly challenged, never honestly explained. Yet I defy you to find a speech about identity by a recent politician that does not mention it.

And while the Old Elite remained firmly rooted in the nation, the impulse of suicidal empathy is pushing the New Elite down a very different path. They have embraced a worldview that tears down majority identity but celebrates all minority identities. They will defend every identity and every culture – except their own.

This is all part of the plan. Once you strip moral legitimacy from the majority, you strip away the rationale for preserving its central role in the nation.

This is how the project of demographic replacement unfolds.

A DEADLY VIRTUE

The highest virtue of the New Elite is not loyalty, duty, or preservation but what the Canadian psychologist Gad Saad has called suicidal empathy. The main priority of today's rulers, he notes, is to display an overwhelming and disproportionate amount of compassion towards anybody who is perceived to be a victim, minority, or marginalised.

The term suicidal empathy nicely captures how leaders in the West are pushing us towards national suicide by feeling limitless empathy and compassion for people who often show none to us in return.

Gad Saad describes it as a 'misfiring of empathy' – a noble emotion hijacked and weaponised against the civilisation that produced it. Empathy, under normal circumstances, is a positive human trait that should be welcomed. But the suicidal empathy that has taken hold of the ruling class has become disconnected from all reason and spiralled out of control.

It is not normal compassion. It is not ordinary kindness. It is an unconditional compassion for outsiders and minorities that pushes leaders to sacrifice their own people and nations. Even worse: they do it in the name of 'moral progress'.

Put plainly, suicidal empathy does three things. First, it elevates outsiders above insiders, turning them into the ultimate moral priority, no matter how they behave or what they believe.

Second, it judges every issue through the lens of victimhood – in terms of who looks most victimised, weak, or marginalised – never through the lens of duty, reciprocity, or loyalty to the nation.

And third, it condemns any attempt by the majority to defend its own interests and even survival as immoral, if not racist and hateful.

Put together, these misfires create the perfect climate for demographic replacement: outsiders are prioritised, insiders are paralysed and any attempt to conserve the majority becomes a moral crime.

Gad Saad's warning is grounded in experience. He grew up as a Jew in Lebanon, in a country torn apart by sectarian politics. He saw first-hand what happens when leaders abandon realism. His family were badly persecuted and fled Lebanon to escape a civil war.

Shaped by these horrors, his warning to the West is simple: 'bad ideas can destroy a civilisation from within.' He is right to say so.

WHAT IT MEANS FOR YOU

What does this bad idea mean for you? It is one thing for a politician to praise 'compassion' and 'empathy' from the comfort of a television studio. It is another thing entirely when that compassion becomes a principle used to justify extreme policies that make the British people's lives harder, less secure and undeniably more dangerous.

I want to emphasise again that this is not the fault of immigrants seeking a better life. It is the fault of a ruling class that invited them in at unprecedented scale, failed to integrate them properly and smeared its own people as immoral for daring to notice the consequences.

In Britain, suicidal empathy means watching leaders consistently elevate a rotating cast of victims, minorities and outsiders above the very people they are meant to protect. It means watching politicians impose extreme policies like mass immigration that are fast-tracking the demographic replacement of the majority, draining the economy, and destabilising the nation – all in the name of 'showing compassion to others'.

It means witnessing the state prising open the borders and deliberately looking the other way as hundreds of thousands of unvetted illegal migrants pour into the country. Some of these arrivals have later been revealed as terrorists, murderers and rapists. Yet the ruling class ploughs on, determined to show 'compassion' and 'empathy' to newcomers while disregarding their own people's right to a secure and safe home.

The same mindset drives the failure to control illegal immigration, which is imposing billions of pounds in costs on taxpayers through endless hotel bills, legal appeals and welfare. It can be seen in how the political class now interprets virtually every question of public policy through the lens of how it affects groups that are deemed to be marginalised, even when those groups include people who have no legal right to be in Britain.

Time and time again, the hard-working, law-abiding majority is expected to pay the financial, cultural and social costs of these decisions, while anybody who questions or criticises these choices is presented as morally deficient.

Suicidal empathy can also be seen in how the political class insist that British taxpayers – while grappling with the worst cost-of-living crisis since the Second World War – must continue to bankroll enormous foreign aid projects that deliver little benefit at home.

Such as forcing the British people to spend £52 million on a road in the South American nation of Guyana, which leads nowhere, £110 million on family planning in Pakistan, or £69 million handing out condoms in the Congo with the aim of 'slowing deforestation'.

At a time when many British families are struggling to heat their homes, the new elite appear more concerned with displaying moral virtue on the world stage than with supporting their own citizens here in Britain.

Another example of this warped mindset is our spiralling welfare state. Britain's welfare bill is projected to exceed £400 billion a year by 2030. Nearly 8.5 million people rely on Universal Credit welfare, nearly half of whom are not even required to look for work, while almost 500 immigrants sign up for welfare every day.

Suicidal empathy is forcing your own people to pay £10 billion every year providing welfare to more than 1.2 million foreign nationals – enough to cover the annual salaries of

250,000 police officers – while sending the tax burden on your own people to record highs.

The British worker is now forced to fund an entirely new demographic bargain: a shrinking productive majority of native-born workers having to pay the bills for an expanding population of dependants, many of whom only recently arrived in the country. This is not a sustainable foundation for any nation, and certainly not for one that is already in decline.

The same mindset is at work in our housing crisis, where the British taxpayer now spends an estimated £6 billion a year sub-sidising social housing – often in prime areas of major cities – for foreign-born households, while British families, young people and veterans have to wait years for a suitable home. It can be seen, too, in foreign policy decisions, such as the plan to hand tens of billions of pounds to the government of Mauritius for a lease on the Chagos Islands, territory that our country already owned.

And it is unmistakable in the extreme Net Zero agenda which has left the British public with the highest industrial energy prices in the developed world while forcing them to pay tens of thou-sands of pounds to replace boilers, install heat pumps, or drive through controlled zones in their cities as the government refuses to expand domestic energy production.

Consistently, a morally righteous ruling class prioritises its own pet projects ahead of what is in the best interests of its own people. It is spending hundreds of billions of pounds on Net Zero, foreign aid, foreign criminals, welfare for foreign nationals and migrants who are breaking our laws, running up an enormous national debt that is costing the British people more than £100 billion a year in payments that are just servicing the *interest* on this debt.

Suicidal empathy can even be found in the justice system, where the New Elite's soft-on-crime policies allow serious offenders to serve only 40% of their sentences, leaving the decent, law-abiding majority living in fear.

It is there, too, in the elevation of transgender ideology above basic biological reality, where male offenders are placed into women's prisons and biological men are permitted into female changing rooms, refuges and sports, all in the name of showing 'compassion' to a sexual minority.

And it is there in the erosion of free speech and individual liberty, in how the ruling class have rolled out a draconian regime of hate laws, online censorship and a definition of 'anti-Muslim hostility', in the name of 'protecting minorities from emotional harm'.

Routinely, the New Elite will sacrifice their own people's right to free speech and free expression on the altar of protecting the feelings of immigrants, minorities and outsiders.

Beneath each of these decisions lies the same distorted impulse: a ruling class that has become far more concerned with how its actions appear to vulnerable outsiders than with the safety, dignity and rights of its own people.

For the British people, the outcome is unmistakable. They are treated as second-class members of their own country, expected to accept declining public services, deteriorating living standards, rising costs and growing insecurity, all while being lectured by a remote class about their supposed moral failings.

This is the very outcome that the Roman statesman Cicero warned against two thousand years ago: a state that abandons its duty to its own people invites disorder, resentment and eventual collapse.

And while the ruling class insists it is acting out of 'kindness', it is often the poorest and most vulnerable families – many of them minorities themselves – who suffer the most from the consequences of this warped ideology.

This is the real meaning of suicidal empathy: a political morality so distorted that it harms not only the historic majority but the entire nation.

Why have elites embraced this worldview? Because for them it is the ultimate luxury belief – a means through which they can display their sense of moral superiority and virtue to other elites while distancing themselves from the supposedly morally inferior people.

One person who foresaw the problems that would come was Sir Roger Scruton. 'No political order', he wrote, 'can achieve stability if it cannot call upon a shared loyalty, a "first-person plural" that distinguishes those who share the benefits and burdens of citizenship from those who are outside the fold'. Today, the ruling class has replaced this shared sense of national loyalty with competitive displays of extravagant sympathy for strangers, even ones who terrorise, murder, rape and assault their own people.

Theirs is a worldview that neither the Old Elite nor our ancestors would recognise. It is how countries collapse from within.

SEIZING CONTROL

How did suicidal empathy become so deeply entrenched? Because the New Elite followed the exact playbook outlined by the Marxist thinker Antonio Gramsci: they captured the institutions. And, as the academic James Burnham once warned, as soon as this woke managerial class had taken full control of the institutions, their interests no longer reflected the interests of the people around them. Increasingly, both the New Elite and the institutions they control withdrew and turned away from the country around them.

Today, it is the New Elite who control the organisations. Look at the evidence. In 2025, a survey by pollsters Find Out Now and Electoral Calculus found that 75% of people working in Britain's key institutions – the civil service, schools, universities, media, creative industries – are on the political left and hold views that are radically at odds with the public.

They are far more likely to believe that minorities should be prioritised over the majority. That Britain's history is a source of shame. That women can become men, or men can become women. And that the majority's free speech should be restricted if it upsets minorities.

The very people who control power are the ones who view public opposition to mass immigration, broken borders and concern about the fate of the majority as shameful moral crimes. These are not neutral beliefs; they are ideological instructions.

Once they seep into our schools, universities, media, museums, galleries, courts, newsrooms, publishers and creative industries, the country begins to systematically turn against the majority. Our institutions become a perfect Petri dish for this new moral virus, reshaped around the belief that the majority must be morally disarmed while outsiders, victims and minorities must be endlessly indulged.

Once this core belief sits inside those institutions, which are themselves often funded by taxpayers, every decision about our borders, immigration policy, welfare, policing, housing and more starts to tilt in the same direction: towards the interests of minorities and away from the forgotten majority. Bad ideas become 'mental parasites', as Gad Saad puts it, spreading until they reshape reality.

This capturing of the institutions is not an end. It is the mechanism that enables the entire project to change not just Britain's values but its population. When elites who worship suicidal empathy control who comes into the country, who can stay, who becomes a citizen and who is allowed to speak about it, then replacing the majority ceases to be a possibility; it becomes an inevitability. It is no longer an accident; it is now the logical outcome of the ideas trickling down from the top.

Now that you understand the ideology driving this transformation, the next question is obvious: how do these ideas translate into concrete demographic change? How do they change not just how we talk about the country or which flags we fly but who the country is *for* – and who is it *made of*? The answer is simple and devastating. It paves the way for the very deliberate and very extreme policy that we explore in the next chapter.

Mass uncontrolled immigration.

CHAPTER THREE

MASS UNCONTROLLED IMMIGRATION

If one day marks the beginning of the project to demographically replace Britain's historic majority, it is Friday 2 May 1997. 'A new dawn has broken, has it not?', Tony Blair triumphantly asked as Britain's newly elected Labour Prime Minister.

It was not just a new government. It was the start of an unprecedented experiment that can be summed up in three words: mass uncontrolled immigration.

Over the next thirty years, this extreme policy would not be justified by any rational assessment of the costs and benefits to the British people or their economy. Nor would it have any democratic consent from the British people. Instead, it would be justified by the new moral creed in Westminster that we examined in the previous chapter – suicidal empathy – the belief that showing limitless compassion to outsiders is morally superior to protecting one's own people. What began was one of the most dangerous experiments to have ever been conducted on a country – an extreme, unchecked re-engineering of a society and its people, carried out without democratic consent and without honest debate.

A BIPARTISAN BETRAYAL

Mass immigration was unlike any other issue in Westminster. It did not divide left and right, it united them. Over the next three decades, both Labour and the Conservatives pursued demographic change on a scale without precedent in Britain's long history.

Why? Because they both absorbed the same elite morality – the belief that to restrict immigration is 'cruel', but to unleash it – no matter the consequences – is 'compassion'.

From 1997 onwards, the policy transformed large parts of the country beyond recognition and in some ways that are nearly impossible to reverse, which makes the betrayal even more sinister.

Between Tony Blair taking power in 1997 and Boris Johnson leaving office twenty-five years later, more than sixteen million immigrants migrated into Britain. While some left, more than eight million, net, were added to the country.

All the while, the ruling class misled, gaslit and lied to the very people who had given them power. They insisted that this churn and change was entirely normal, fully in keeping with our history. It was nothing of the kind.

To grasp how radical a rupture this was, consider one fact. In *each* year after 1997, Britain experienced more immigration than it had during the *combined* 1,500 years between the Anglo-Saxons in the fifth century and the end of the Second World War.

Until 1997, Britain had simply not been a country of mass immigration and rapid demographic change. From that moment onwards, the New Elite took it upon themselves to redefine the country, elevating their suicidal empathy over what a previous ruling class had once viewed as its sacred duty: preserving national continuity.

Borders were no longer seen as tools of statecraft and self-defence but as symbols of cruelty to be relaxed or removed. Diversity became synonymous with virtue. To oppose it was immoral; to question it was bigotry; to accelerate it was now a moral obligation.

Motivated by their ideology and intense hunger for social status and applause from other elites, they opened the floodgates and set the stage for Britain's transformation.

The policy unfolded in three phases: New Labour's decision to usher in this policy between 1997 and 2010; the Tory party's decision to make this revolution permanent between 2010 and 2019; and then Boris Johnson's decision, after 2019, to put it on steroids through the 'Boriswave', a tsunami of migration that dwarfed all that came before.

What remains is what you see around you today: a country that no longer looks or feels like the one you grew up in, and a historic majority hurtling towards its own eclipse.

THE BLAIRITE REVOLUTION

When Tony Blair and New Labour took office, net migration into Britain had averaged around 50,000 people a year, meaning 50,000 more people coming than leaving.

By historic standards that was already high. Between 1951 and 2001, the average had been 8,000 a year and often negative, with more leaving the country than arriving.

Within a few years of Blair entering Downing Street, those numbers rocketed into the stratosphere. Within a decade, roughly eight million migrants, many from outside Europe, flooded into Britain and brought radically different cultures and beliefs with them.

This was no accident. As Andrew Neather, speechwriter to Tony Blair and his immigration minister Barbara Roche, admitted in 2009, mass immigration had been a deliberate policy. The aim, he said, was to 'rub the Right's nose in diversity'.

Labour strategists also assumed the new arrivals would vote Labour. They were right. Roughly 80% of Muslims voted Labour in 1997, and ever since then Labour have exploited clan-based networks in minority communities to deliver blocs of votes, turning a blind eye to the sectarianism they were now importing into British politics.

New Labour loosened visa rules across the board – relaxing spousal routes, turning a blind eye to visa overstayers, expanding student visas and opening the door to masses of cheap migrant workers from poorer nations in Eastern Europe.

A party that was founded to defend labour quietly entered

into an alliance with global capital to undermine it. Corporations wanted a permanent supply of cheap workers; Labour elites wanted to bask in their own moral largesse.

What made this alliance possible was suicidal empathy, an elite ideology that treated loyalty to outsiders as the highest moral good, even when British workers paid the price.

Global firms, like the ruling class, became addicted to mass migration. It kept wages down, profits up and demand for goods and services high, no matter the impact on British people.

The British state, meanwhile, proved utterly incompetent. Civil servants originally forecast that just 13,000 workers from Europe would move to Britain. In reality, around 1.3 million came.

Tony Blair's Human Rights Act, which entrenched the European Convention on Human Rights into UK law, made matters even worse. Asylum seekers, illegal migrants, foreign criminals and the activist lawyers who defended them now had a powerful new tool to resist their deportation. From here on, the British people would find it virtually impossible to control their own borders and laws.

Because of these changes, net migration soon exceeded 200,000 a year, levels never before seen. By the time New Labour was removed from power, in 2010, 3.5 million migrants had been added to the country, net, despite nobody ever voting for this to happen and despite it appearing in no party manifesto.

A 'BIGOTED' PEOPLE

For the New Elite, this was all a triumph. They celebrated supposed gains for cosmopolitan degree holders like themselves and spoke endlessly about the moral nobility of 'openness'.

They had much less to say about the people whose lives were transformed without consent. Those who questioned or criticised the policy were showered with contempt. The same politicians who preached empathy for outsiders showed none for their own people.

Tony Blair's successor, Gordon Brown, briefly toyed with acknowledging the people's concerns, promising 'British jobs for British workers'. But the mask slipped in Rochdale, in April 2010, a town that would later come to symbolise the disaster of mass immigration when a huge Pakistani rape gang was uncovered.

There, Gillian Duffy, a sixty-five-year-old widow and life-long Labour voter, challenged Brown about debt and immigration. Brown smiled and nodded. She described him as a very nice man. But once he had returned to his Jaguar – still wired to a Sky News microphone – he was heard to dismiss her as a 'bigoted woman'.

The remark appeared to confirm what millions already suspected: the people who were supposed to represent them privately despised them. Scepticism about immigration was not treated as a legitimate concern but as a moral failing.

Suicidal empathy had taught Britain's elites that compassion for outsiders trumped obligations to their own. Eight days later, Brown and Labour were swept out of office.

Despite mass immigration being one of his most consequential legacies, Blair said almost nothing about it after leaving office. In a 700-page autobiography, he devoted barely a couple of pages to the subject, brushing off public concern as 'emotional' and presenting the policy as 'inevitable' when it was no such thing.

What he never admitted was the most important truth of all: the British people – including those being pushed into their own demographic replacement – were never asked.

THE SECOND PHASE

The second phase of the policy began in 2010, with successive Conservative governments that promised change but delivered continuity.

David Cameron and his 'modernising' Conservatives – who even called themselves 'progressive conservatives' – pledged to cut net migration to the 'tens of thousands'.

They did nothing of the sort.

They, too, had absorbed the morality of the New Elite. To refuse mass immigration was to risk being called 'racist' or 'nasty' at dinner parties for the BBC/Westminster set. To endorse it was to signal virtue in front of journalists, NGOs, business leaders and the global class whose applause they craved.

Conservatives were also more interested in placating their donor class in the City than defending their voters. Global corporations still wanted cheap labour; the Tories obliged. The interests of the British people were once again brushed aside.

The fact that the new era of mass immigration coincided with weak economic growth, stagnant or falling GDP per capita and declining living standards was politely ignored. It clashed with the story elites now told themselves and the country – that Britain's moral worth and economic strength depended on ever-higher inflows of migrants.

They were more than happy to sacrifice the British people's living standards on the altar of a policy that fed their own moral righteousness. No matter what their manifestoes said, no matter what the public demanded, mass immigration was now locked in.

Net migration continued to climb to astonishing levels: 256,000 a year in 2010 – roughly the population of Portsmouth – rising to 303,000 in 2015, equivalent to adding the population of Newcastle upon Tyne in just one year.

When the people rebelled in the 2016 referendum, voting for Brexit in large part to try and lower immigration and slow the pace of change, the ruling class refused to listen.

Brexit voters were promptly denounced as 'racists', 'far-right', and 'gammons', so-called, it was claimed, because their faces turn red with rage when sharing their views. Commentators, meanwhile, sought to distract people from the real motivation by blaming Russia, social media and alleged 'misinformation' among voters.

Anything to avoid admitting the obvious: the British people wanted lower immigration, slower demographic change and a chance to preserve their nation.

Brexit, the clearest democratic instruction in modern British history, was treated not as a mandate but as a grave mistake. And so, the politicians carried on.

Throughout the 2010s, under the very Tory party that had been founded to conserve the country, another five million migrants were added to its population, net.

It was now undeniable: whatever the British people wanted, their language, identity, culture and way of life were being radically transformed by a political class that insisted it knew best. The numbers of immigrants were vast, scarcely believable, unlike anything Britain had seen before. And yet, as staggering as they were, they would soon look modest next to the tidal wave that was coming.

THE BORISWAVE

If you had to identify one person who did more than any other to fast-track the demographic replacement of Britain's historic majority, it would not be a Labour politician. It would be a Conservative: Boris Johnson.

In only a few years, Boris Johnson did far more than Tony Blair, Gordon Brown, or any of his other predecessors to divide and destabilise Britain.

The man who modelled himself on Winston Churchill, who famously waved two Union Jacks from a zip wire during the 2012 Olympics, presided over a colossal betrayal of the British people.

Boris Johnson did not merely maintain the existing system; he turbo-charged it, despite promising he would do the very opposite. He wrapped record-breaking immigration in the feel-good language of humanitarianism and 'Global Britain', turning suicidal empathy into official policy. Britain's moral worth continued to be measured not by how it treated its own people but rather by how many immigrants it could absorb.

Before the 2019 general election, Boris Johnson had pledged 'lower overall numbers' and 'control of the borders'. Once in office, he and his Home Secretary Priti Patel delivered the largest wave of immigration in Britain's history, much of it from outside Europe.

They did not just change the numbers; they changed the composition, structure and character of the country. By the time they were done, 80% of all immigration into Britain came from outside Europe, from radically different cultures.

No serious thought was given to the social fabric of the country – to integration, cohesion, housing, or pressures on public services. No respect was shown to the millions of ordinary people who would now have to live with the consequences.

Johnson liberalised the entire system and moved to redefine Britain in his own globalist image. He scrapped a previous cap on migrant workers from outside Europe. He opened routes for low-skill workers. He reduced educational requirements for immigrants arriving. He slashed salary thresholds to just £25,600, or less in many sectors. He brought back a post-study work visa for foreign students, allowing them to stay in Britain after they had finished their study. He allowed the relatives of care workers and students to pour in. He issued humanitarian visas with no meaningful caps.

Most telling of all, he even removed the requirement for firms to advertise jobs to British workers before recruiting overseas. In one stroke, he signalled where his loyalties truly lay: not with British labour, but with global capital and the New Elite.

THE OPENING OF THE FLOODGATES

The results were devastating.

Net migration, which had stood at 184,000 in 2019, exploded to 467,000 in 2021, 891,000 in 2022, 944,000 in 2023 and then another 345,000 in 2024, higher than anything that had been seen before Brexit.

In less than four years, Johnson added three million immigrants, net, to Britain's population. The total inflows were even more staggering: nearly one million immigrants in 2021, 1.4 million in 2022, over 1.4 million in 2023 and another million in 2024.

Between January 2021 and December 2024, roughly 4.2 million migrants moved to Britain, equivalent to adding the combined populations of Birmingham, Manchester and Glasgow, or the entire nation of Croatia.

That figure, 4.2 million, is eerily close to the £3.8 million Johnson later spent on a well-protected manor house in Oxfordshire, in a village that is 98% white. The man who unleashed unprecedented demographic change on the British people despite nobody ever voting for it then chose to retreat to one of the whitest, safest corners of the country.

In fact, the Boriswave was so immense that one in every twenty-five people living in Britain today arrived in the last four years. The biggest population surge on record was imposed on the country without any democratic mandate.

While Johnson spoke of attracting 'the best and the brightest', this, too, was a brazen lie. In reality, both he and the Tories hollowed out Britain's economy in the name of a feel-good morality. They flooded Britain with waves of low-wage, low-skill, poorly educated migrant workers from outside Europe who, as even the government's own officials would later concede, have become a net fiscal drain on the economy and British taxpayers.

This was suicidal empathy masquerading as economic strategy: a political class so desperate to appear compassionate, so eager to please global business, that it sacrificed British workers, depressed wages and left taxpayers with an enormous bill.

'BEST AND BRIGHTEST'

As experts such as Karl Williams, Research Director at the Centre of Policy Studies, have shown, by 2024, the claim that this policy was boosting Britain's economy was laughable.

Of the millions of visas that were issued under Boris Johnson's regime, only about 12% went to skilled workers; most of whom were in low-paid roles that cost more than they contributed to the economy.

Britain did not receive the wave of brilliant engineers, entrepreneurs, or scientists that Boris Johnson promised. It was transformed, instead, into a 'Deliveroo Economy': masses of poorly paid drivers, couriers and gig workers, often with limited English, drawn from cultures completely different from our own.

The New Elite did not care. For them, sacrificing Britain's prosperity on the altar of suicidal empathy is now a virtue. What mattered was not building a productive economy that supported the tax-paying British majority but displaying compassion to outsiders.

The grim reality was simply ignored, such as the fact that the country was not only being flooded with low-skill workers who were a net fiscal cost but hundreds of thousands of their relatives, who were a further drain on the economy and British taxpayers.

Between 2021 and 2024, astonishingly, Britain issued nearly 700,000 health and social care visas, of which 410,000 – almost 60% – went not to workers but their relatives.

In the early months of 2024, Britain granted 1,063 health and care visas to people from Zimbabwe – and 10,670 visas to their relatives. Ten relatives for every worker.

None of it made any sense.

Civil servants also clearly had no idea what they were unleashing. They had expected some 6,000 migrants a year to come on the health and care route. Between 2021 and 2024, nearly 650,000 came – roughly 270,000 workers and 377,000 relatives.

Even the government's own data later revealed that most of these relatives were not working, and when they were working they were often in low-paid roles, earning below the median wage and hence imposing further net costs on British taxpayers.

In late 2025, for instance, the Migration Advisory Committee revealed that the relatives of migrants – most of whom were not working – had generated £5.6 billion in costs for the hard-working British people who had never voted for this policy in the first place.

Each relative, they noted, costs roughly £109,000 over the course of their lifetime, about the same amount as the average British resident contributes. As the British people pay into the collective pot, in other words, many migrants and their families take money out, reflecting a system that makes zero economic sense.

Britain's health and social care sector also became rife with fraud and corruption, with significant numbers of migrants openly gaming the system. One social care provider was found to have sponsored 498 visas despite no longer providing any services.

A test centre in Nigeria provided fake qualifications. At least 2% of Nigerians on the health and social care visa were later found to have fraudulent credentials, yet some were still made responsible for nursing and midwifery. Nobody seemed to be in control.

By 2025, the legacy of Boris Johnson's insane immigration system remained on display when official figures confirmed that of the 871,000 visas that had been issued the previous year barely one in five had gone to work applicants. The rest had gone to foreign students, relatives, asylum seekers and refugees, with nearly 50,000 illegal migrants on top.

This is suicidal empathy in its purest form: a ruling class so desperate to signal compassion that it opened the door to masses of low-skill migrants who are a net fiscal cost and vast numbers of their dependants, who the country now also had to support.

Another powerful example of this failing policy is what has happened in the National Health Service, where mass immigration has also been used by the ruling class to undermine and sideline the British people.

The fashionable claim that the Boriswave of immigration was needed to 'save our NHS' was always misleading. Of the 4.3

million visas that were handed out during this time, only about one in forty went to doctors or nurses.

But the bigger picture is even more troubling. For decades, Britain's politicians have preferred to import foreign doctors rather than train young British people. Such is their addiction to this that in 2025 it was revealed the country has twice as many foreign doctors and nurses as the Western average, with foreign-trained doctors making up nearly 42% of the medical workforce, compared to only 15% in Germany and 11% in France.

At the same time, each year, British medical schools turn away thousands of qualified young British students because the ruling class believe that training our own doctors and nurses is 'too expensive'. The perversity is truly astonishing.

In 2024, Britain produced just over 9,000 trained doctors yet registered nearly 20,000 from overseas, including roughly 17,000 from poorer nations such as India, Pakistan, Nigeria and Bangladesh, countries whose own health systems are under enormous strain and where training standards are lower. In 2025, *The Times* reported that many doctors who had been banned from practising overseas were still approved to treat British patients.

Then, many of these foreign medics take limited speciality training places within the NHS, forcing the dwindling number of our own doctors, nurses and anaesthetists, who have been subsidised by the taxpayer, to flee to countries like Australia.

Suicidal empathy lies at the heart of this madness: the belief that relying on imported labour is morally superior to investing in one's own people. British students are shut out. British taxpayers are forced to pick up the bill. Poorer countries lose their desperately needed clinicians. And the ruling class here in Britain congratulates itself on its 'compassion'.

Even worse, politicians then force the British people to send tens of billions of pounds in foreign aid to the same poor countries they are simultaneously poaching doctors from while eroding the prospects of British students and British-trained clinicians.

In this way, the hardworking, tax-paying majority – people from the 'alarm clock class' who have to set their alarms and get up in the morning to keep the country running – have to subsidise a broken immigration system and, increasingly, their own replacement.

We see this, too, in the national welfare state, which has been transformed by the ruling class into an international welfare regime. That is the inevitable endpoint of suicidal empathy: a system built for national citizens becomes a system for the world.

In 2025, freedom of information requests – which had to be fought for because the state that lectures the public about 'misinformation' refuses to share it – revealed that more than £10.1 billion in Universal Credit welfare payments – fully one pound in every six paid out – now goes to claimants who were not even born in Britain.

More than 1.24 million foreign-born residents receive welfare payments. Between 2022 and 2024 alone, payments to households that contain at least one Pakistani national surged from £430 million to £700 million.

All this unfolded as the British people were learning of the full horror of the Pakistani Muslim rape gang scandal – the systematic rape of vulnerable White British working-class girls by organised gangs, and the years of silence, denial and evasion by officials too frightened of being called 'racist' to defend the children they are paid to protect.

Boris Johnson and the Tories not only presided over much of this mess; they also flooded Britain with enormous numbers of international students, many of whom enrolled on dubious courses at failing universities that should have been closed.

Fraud flourished. Many foreign students gamed the system, using student visas to get into Britain only to then switch onto other visas or disappear into the black economy.

I know this because I was a university academic for twenty years. I was often told not to fail international students because cash-strapped universities desperately needed their higher rate of international student fees. In this way, the system erodes itself from within, as academic standards and excellence are downgraded in the pursuit of international fees.

While all this was happening, under both Labour and the Tories, the politicians said virtually nothing about the estimated 9.2 million working-age Britons who are economically inactive, including more than a million young people who are not in education, employment or training. They are simply not a priority in Westminster.

Instead of investing in the forgotten majority, Labour and Tory politicians constantly reached for the lazy substitute of mass immigration, putting moral vanity, their suicidal empathy and corporate demands ahead of their own people.

The financial cost of all this has been colossal. In 2024, the Office for Budget Responsibility (OBR) quietly confirmed what many suspected: each low-wage migrant worker is a net fiscal drain on the country from the moment they arrive. By the time they reach the age of eighty-one, each one will cost the taxpayer £465,000.

The state knows this yet presses on regardless. Studies in Denmark, Finland and the Netherlands have found the same: low-wage, low-skill migrants from outside Europe take more out of the system than they put in, while also eroding the social trust and shared identity a nation needs to endure.[13]

The true bill for the Boriswave will be far higher than current estimates. From 2026, many of the migrants who arrived in Britain after 2021 will qualify for something called 'Indefinite Leave to Remain'. This will grant them permanent residence, full access to the welfare state, student loans, the NHS and the right to bring in relatives – all without the British people ever having agreed to it. Some think tanks in Westminster estimate that the eventual cost of all this to the British people could soon exceed £200 billion.

THE POPULATION TRAP

Whenever concerns about this issue are raised, the ruling class deploy a familiar line: 'We need immigration to deal with our ageing society.' But this, too, is deeply misleading.

As we have seen, much research has already shown that the kind of immigration policy that is being pursued in Britain is a net fiscal cost, not a benefit. Furthermore, as Professor David Miles from the Office for Budget Responsibility has suggested, relying on ever-higher immigration and an ever-expanding population to support a growing elderly population simply does not work.

For a start, migrants themselves age, draw pensions, use public services, require housing, bring relatives, have children, and claim welfare benefits. Also, to keep the ratio of workers to pensioners stable, you must keep increasing the inflow. This is why David Miles estimates that Britain would need around *twenty million* additional migrants to balance the numbers, pushing the population towards one hundred million by 2064.

This is not a policy; it is a nightmare. Housing, roads, hospitals, schools, the environment and social cohesion would all buckle.

It is what experts call a 'Population Trap': once a country depends on relentless mass immigration, it can never step off the treadmill without a massive fiscal shock. The speed and scale of demographic change become so great that the state can no longer carry out its basic duties – securing borders, maintaining affordable housing, providing high-quality healthcare, upholding law and order.

There is another way. Britain could bring millions of its own economically inactive people back into work. It could create serious incentives for British families to have more children. It could build affordable housing that is kept aside for British young people and professionals who are working, so that they can start families and have more children. It could no longer spend billions of pounds on welfare support for people who are not British and instead plough this money into frontline public services for the British people.

Other countries grasp the importance of these things and the wider goal of demographic continuity. Hungary, Israel and Poland treat fertility as a national priority and control immigration accordingly. In Britain, by contrast, suicidal empathy means the needs of new arrivals routinely trump the needs of the people who built the country.

This has also had other insidious effects. The policy of mass immigration has not just strained public services, it has eroded our shared identity, culture, values and way of life. And because it has been imposed without the people's consent, it has shattered trust in politics.

In her work, academic Lauren McLaren has shown how repeated failures to control immigration – including the refusal even to take public concerns seriously – have led to a collapse of trust in not just political parties but the entire political system.

Whenever voters are given a say, they demand lower immigration and slower demographic change. But their rulers have ignored them and pressed ahead, transforming their home into a place their parents and grandparents would barely recognise.

CULTURE TRANSPLANT

Most fundamentally, mass immigration has also transformed the composition of the country. If you replace the majority group of a nation you are essentially replacing the nation. You might call it by the same name, but it is no longer really the same nation.

This is precisely what mass immigration is doing to the White British majority. It is hastening the decline of the historic majority. Without this historic core, as Professor Anthony Smith warned, the nation loses its distinctive identity and becomes an empty shell.

What also matters here is exactly who is being brought into the country. By 2023, thanks to the changes introduced by Labour and the Tories and turbo-charged by Boris Johnson, roughly four-fifths of all the immigrants arriving in Britain came from outside Europe, from cultures far removed from our own.

In 2025, of the 835,000 visas that were granted to foreign nationals, the most common nationalities were Indians, Chinese, Pakistanis and Nigerians. More than half the Boriswave consisted of migrants from outside Europe – typically from India, Nigeria, China, Pakistan, Ukraine, Bangladesh, Zimbabwe, Ghana and Nepal.

Our ties to Europe and the Anglosphere, in other words, have been weakened, while our ties with countries that are neither developed nor Western have deepened.

Many of these new arrivals, as we have already seen, do not speak English well. Large numbers identify more with their religious community – particularly Islam – or with their country of origin than with Britain's national identity.

One economist who has been honest about what this means is Garett Jones, author of *The Culture Transplant*, published in 2022. When people cross borders, he shows, they do not arrive as blank slates. They bring their cultures, norms and institutions with them. 'When a nation imports people', he writes, 'it imports the average cultural traits of those people.'

Cultures do not get left at the border and do not dissolve quickly. They persist for generations, shaping the host country's politics, economy and civic life.

Sometimes, of course, this can be positive. Garett Jones points to the Huguenots, for example, who were highly skilled Protestant refugees from France who fled persecution in the seventeenth century. Culturally compatible and productive, they strengthened Britain's industries and fitted easily into the national story.

But the kind of immigration that Britain is experiencing today is very different from the Huguenots in the seventeenth century. Millions are now arriving from countries that are marked by deep ethnic and religious divisions, low social trust, weak institutions and very different attitudes to crime, sexuality, the family and religion.

Suicidal empathy refuses to distinguish between culturally compatible and culturally incompatible migration. It treats all inflows as equally virtuous, whatever the consequences.

The most horrific example of what happens when this transfer of cultures goes badly wrong is the Pakistani Muslim rape gang scandal, which, as we will see in the pages to come, saw clan-based networks from Pakistan systematically abuse vulnerable non-Muslim girls.

The key point is that the demographic changes that have been unleashed on Britain by elites in Westminster are not only undermining the economy; they are also now reshaping our national culture, or what Sir Roger Scruton once called our 'delicate spirit'.

As mass immigration continues to import into Britain radically different cultures from outside Europe, the core of the nation is being gradually weakened and will, eventually, give way altogether. And as that core is replaced, so, too, eventually, is the nation itself.

THE COMING WAVE

Unless Britain urgently changes course, all of the shifts that I am pointing to will intensify.

In 2025, the Office for National Statistics projected that net migration will add another 6.1 million people to the country by the year 2036.

Between 2021 and 2036, on current trends, nearly fourteen million more people are expected to move to Britain, with 7.6 million leaving, which is equivalent to adding a new city three times the size of Greater Manchester to the country. This is on top of what has already arrived over the previous thirty years.

At the same time, a growing number of British people are leaving for good. In 2025, around 257,000 British citizens emigrated – many young people in their twenties and thirties who have concluded for the reasons I have pointed to that Britain no longer treats them fairly.

Britain is losing high-skill professionals, including many of its own doctors and nurses, to America, Australia, Dubai and Italy and replacing them with low-skill, low-wage and poorly educated workers from outside Europe who impose enormous costs.

Despite constant talk in Westminster about 'reducing numbers', official projections by government departments quietly assume that Britain will have an ongoing rate of net migration of at least 340,000 a year, which is higher than before Brexit and far beyond anything seen for most of our history.

What we are left with is an astonishing pace of change. It took fifty-five years, from 1950 to 2005, for the population to grow from fifty to sixty million. It will take less than half that time, from 2005 to 2026, to surge from sixty to seventy million, with much of that growth due to immigration from across the Middle East, Africa and Asia.

The Office for National Statistics has even started mapping what this means locally. By 2047, net migration is expected to add another 307,000 people to Birmingham, 273,000 to Manchester, 267,000 to Newham, 236,000 to Coventry and roughly 200,000 in Tower Hamlets, Leicester, Leeds and Sheffield.

On current trends, by 2046, migrants who arrived in the last twenty-five years will account for more than half the populations of Cambridge and Leicester, over 40% of Manchester, Nottingham, Welwyn and Hatfield and Luton, more than a third of Southampton, Middlesbrough, Reading and Newcastle and more than a quarter of Exeter, Preston, Sheffield, Portsmouth, Liverpool and Birmingham.

What gives a nation its character, as scholars such as Anthony Smith have pointed out, is not just institutions, borders and legal documents, but shared myths, memories and symbols. However, demographic change at this speed and scale will simply blow these myths and memories apart. What lies ahead will not be gentle evolution – the kind of manageable change that ensures a nation's survival – but a deliberate, radical, engineered transformation.

And at every stage, the engineers have justified themselves with the same refrain: empathy, compassion and moral superiority demanded it.

THE LUXURY BELIEF CLASS

While the British people have been left to grapple with the effects of this extreme policy, its architects have flourished. Tony Blair and Boris Johnson have both become classic examples of what the writer Rob Henderson has called the 'Luxury Belief Class' – elites who promote extreme ideas whose costs they never personally pay.

For Blair, the rewards have been global consultancy and lucrative deals with foreign governments. For Johnson, they have included a multi-million pound manor in Oxfordshire and millions in speaking fees from banks and conglomerates.

Blair and Johnson belong to different political parties but they clearly share the same attitude to the people whose lives they have transformed: distant, dismissive, contemptuous.

Twenty-five years of mass immigration have turned a stable, integrated majority nation into a fragmented, chaotic and unstable one, a country that is now racing towards a future in which its historic majority becomes just another group among many.

Britain was never a 'nation of immigrants' and was certainly not 'built by immigrants'. But unless we change course, it will soon have been remade by mass immigration, not by chance, but by the deliberate choices of a remote ruling class.

Millions who live with the effects of this policy can feel what is happening. The country they once knew is slipping away and being replaced by something unrecognisable.

And, as we will see in the next chapter, much of this is now also being compounded by something else: the complete collapse of Britain's borders.

CHAPTER FOUR

BROKEN BORDERS

Imagine you were the leader of a country but secretly wanted to destroy it. What would you do?

You would start by breaking its borders. You would refuse to control who comes and who goes. You would impose open borders without any democratic mandate, oversight, or consent from your people. You would allow countless numbers of unvetted young fighting-age men from radically different cultures to enter illegally.

You would never ask them what they believe, or why they broke the law to get here. You would place them not on remote islands while you vet them and process their claims but in the heart of your communities – near families, schools, synagogues, children.

You would do this even while knowing that among those arriving are criminals, rapists and terrorists, and that there is more than a fair chance your own people will be harmed.

You would take money from your own struggling citizens to house, feed and even entertain those who are arriving in the middle of one of the worst cost-of-living crises on record. You would force your citizens to pay millions of pounds each day – *billions* every year – for the privilege of living with a policy they never even asked for to begin with.

You could even go one step further and rig the housing market against your own people: using their money to bankroll private companies that offer better contracts to landlords who rent their homes to illegal migrants instead of to British families.

While refusing to defend the border, you would work relentlessly to silence dissent, building a regime of censorship that punishes anyone who dares to complain. And when people do object – especially in towns that are haunted by the rape gangs, knife crime, or terrorist plots – you would denounce them as 'far-right', 'racist' and 'hateful'. You would weaponise language and shame to make one thing clear: opposition is not allowed.

This is not fantasy. This is Britain today. This is what the New Elite, gripped by their suicidal empathy, have done to the country. It is what happens when a ruling class stops putting its own citizens first and becomes obsessed with importing foreigners and outsiders in the name of 'compassion' and 'empathy' – even those who despise or harm the people who live here.

It is what happens when politicians refuse to defend the border because they are terrified of being called 'racist' by other elites; and it is what happens when violence, rape and sexual assault committed by foreigners is downplayed or ignored because the same politicians would rather protect their preferred narrative of 'diversity' than protect their own.

In this chapter, we will see how the ruling class is not only driving the demographic replacement of the historic majority through mass legal immigration but is compounding this by allowing illegal migration on a scale past generations would have regarded as unthinkable.

HOW TO MAKE PEOPLE GIVE UP

A country that cannot control its own borders is not a serious country. And a nation that cannot protect its own people will eventually cease to be a nation. That is Britain's condition today. An island nation with every natural advantage has spent thirty years being told by successive governments – Labour and Tory alike – that 'nothing can be done' about illegal migration.

Winston Churchill would have laughed. Margaret Thatcher would have kicked the table over. Yet today, a weary people have been browbeaten into accepting this fiction. It is a demoralising lesson in how a people can be trained to surrender their own sovereignty.

The ruling class shrug while the British people open their newspapers to see tens of thousands of illegal migrants crossing the Channel each year in small boats, almost none of whom are being deported, and all being accommodated, often in luxury hotels, at staggering expense to the taxpayer.

This is not only imposing enormous costs that could have gone into public services or reducing tax. It is weakening our security, eroding trust and tearing up the social contract. It is making a mockery of the idea that Britain is still a sovereign, self-governing country and leaving ordinary people feeling like second-class citizens in their own home.

The American economist Thomas Sowell understood this clearly. 'Immigration laws', he wrote, 'are the only laws that are ever discussed in terms of how to help people who break them.' This is what it feels like to many people in Britain: a governing class that is no longer defending and upholding our laws but prioritising people who break them.

What does that do to public faith in the rule of law? What happens to the British people's famous sense of fair play when those who obey the law are punished while those who break it are rewarded? The answer is simple: people give up. The social contract frays.

The illegal migration crisis that now tears at Britain is not an accident or an unfortunate side effect. Like the policy of mass legal immigration, it is the inevitable outcome of suicidal empathy, a compulsion among elites to place outsiders above their own citizens, even at the cost of chaos, insecurity and death.

THE INVASION FORCE

The numbers are not just astonishing; they are barely believable.

From 2018 to 2025, nearly 200,000 illegal migrants crossed the Channel in small boats, enough to fill a city the size of York. This is more than the combined number serving in the British Army, the Navy and the RAF. It is more than those who took part in the D-Day landings in June 1944.

Add to that the estimated 700,000–900,000 illegal migrants already in the country and a further 180,000 illegal migrants forecast to cross the Channel before the next general election, and Britain could soon have 1.3 million illegal migrants – a city larger than Birmingham.

When they arrive, the British people are then forced to watch open-mouthed as those who are breaking their laws are not marched out but ushered in.

They are handed cash cards, smartphones, medical care, school places, hotel rooms, driving lessons, free public transport and university places.

In the middle of a cost-of-living crisis and deteriorating living standards, taxpayers read about discounts for illegal migrants on martial arts lessons, days out on dinghies and half-price e-bikes – benefits more generous than those offered to British veterans and pensioners.

While the National Health Service is treating British people in corridors and car parks, it issued nearly one million HC2 certificates to asylum seekers and illegal migrants in just five years, entitling them to free prescriptions, eye tests, glasses and contact lenses, dentistry, wigs of three different grades and travel to receive treatment.

Asylum seekers account for 60% of these certificates, which were designed to help British people on low incomes. There is even a taxi service. In 2025, one illegal migrant revealed that after being moved from one hotel to another he ran up a £600 fare for a 250-mile round trip to visit his GP about a sore knee. How is any of this fair, many people ask?

The elites use language to make this appear more acceptable.

They avoid the word 'illegal', preferring the more sanitised term 'irregular migration', as though this were a minor administrative mistake, not the systematic breaching of a sovereign border. But it should be called what it is: an invasion. The *Oxford Dictionary* is clear in its definition: an invasion is 'an unwelcome intrusion into another's domain'.

Who is arriving? Most are young men of fighting age, from countries whose cultures are profoundly different from Britain's: Afghanistan, Iraq, Eritrea, Somalia, Syria and beyond.

Nations that fail to distinguish their citizens from strangers, or which tolerate people who are intolerant toward those nations, will not survive. As Sir Roger Scruton warned in his classic pamphlet, *The Need for Nations*,[14] without strong national loyalties the social contract, which asks us to support people we have not met, will simply collapse. But this is exactly what suicidal empathy has done to our leaders. They are prioritising strangers over their own people.

Clearly, some of those arriving are genuine refugees. But many are not. Among them, Britain's leaders have allowed suspected Iranian terrorists, arrested over an alleged plot to attack the Israeli embassy, and the likes of Fiyaz Khan, a twenty-six-year-old Afghan national found guilty of threatening to kill Nigel Farage, leader of Reform UK. They have also included alleged Islamic State supporters from Iraq, Iran, Afghanistan, Somalia and Libya, and men who we know have gone on to join organised rape gangs.

Back in 2015, European Parliament officials acknowledged Islamist extremists were using migrant boats to flood European nations with potential terrorists. Yet Britain's politicians took no notice, choosing to usher unvetted migrants in and placing them in our communities – all in the name of showing 'compassion' to others. What more evidence does one need for the claim that the New Elite either do not care about their own people or openly despise them?

As the economist Garett Jones reminded us in the last chapter, when a nation imports people it imports the average cultural traits of those people. It is not just bodies that are crossing the Channel; it is expectations, habits, loyalties and norms. If you change the people then you change the nation – and Britain is changing, fast.

Let us speak honestly. Many of the cultures our leaders are importing into Britain are inferior, primitive and hostile to things like women's rights, individual choice and freedom. Many of the people arriving remain stuck in cultural codes, behaviours and lifestyles that Western nations abandoned centuries ago. Our leaders are deluded if they believe that illegal migrants hold the same respect for our laws, customs and citizens as we do.

We should be honest about what the data shows. Freedom of Information requests have forced the truth out of a British state that does not want to tell people the truth. They reveal vast differences in crime rates by nationality, showing that the most common nationalities on the small boats are far more likely than the British people to commit crimes.

Albanians, who make up roughly one in ten foreign prisoners, have the highest arrest rate of any nationality in Britain – 210 arrests for every 1,000 of their people. They are followed by Afghans (a rate of 107), Iraqis (93), Algerians (73), Moroccans (70) and Somalis (65). The rate among British people is 12 for every 1,000.[15]

North Africans are convicted of sexual assault at around *seven times* the rate of British people. Those from the Middle East are convicted at nearly *four times* the rate, and those from Sub-Sahara Africa nearly *three times*. Even more shockingly, Afghans and Eritreans are *twenty times* more likely to be convicted of sexual assault.

Migrants from seven nationalities that made up three-quarters of the small boat arrivals in 2024 – Afghans, Syrians, Iranians, Vietnamese, Eritreans, Sudanese and Iraqis – accounted for a *110%* surge in the number of sexual assault convictions compared with three years earlier.

Why is nobody in the New Elite talking about this? Why do they insist on telling us all cultures are equal? Why must citizens drag this information from the state? Why is the priority always defending the reputation of the policy rather than defending the safety of the people who are forced to pay for it? Nobody in Westminster seems interested in these questions.

WHO PAYS THE PRICE?

The answer to this question is simple: suicidal empathy. The ruling class is so committed to its own moral self-image that it cannot admit the costs its policies impose on real people.

Those costs are borne, overwhelmingly, by ordinary Britons, especially women and girls. Consider the case of Rhiannon Whyte, a twenty-seven-year-old mother from Walsall, murdered by an illegal migrant from Sudan who should never have been in Britain.

Rhiannon was on her way home after a late shift at the Park Inn Hotel, a hotel for asylum seekers. Her generosity was repaid with horror. As she walked to the local railway station, speaking to a friend on her mobile, the line suddenly went silent. Her friend heard only blood-curdling screams. Her attacker, Deng Majek, had been in Britain less than three months. Living at the hotel, he followed Rhiannon, stabbed her twenty-three times with a screwdriver and left her dying. Rhiannon suffered eleven blows to her skull. She died in hospital three days later from catastrophic brain injuries.

After the murder, Majek bought alcohol, threw Rhiannon's phone into a river and was filmed back at the hotel dancing and laughing. In court he appeared bored, pretended not to understand English, lied about his age and showed no remorse. He was one of many criminal migrants our leaders have welcomed under the guise of 'compassion' and 'tolerance'.

Rhiannon's family said she was devoted to helping others. It fell to her sister to inform Rhiannon's five-year-old son his mother had died. 'The scream that left that child that day will haunt me for the rest of my life', said the sister. 'I've never heard a child cry like that, and I never want to hear a child cry like that again.'

Why did Rhiannon die? What is the truth that one day her son will have to be told about the murder of his mother? She was unlucky, yes, but she was also the victim of a political moral code in which the suffering of British women is treated as an acceptable price for elite virtue.

While ever since 2020 politicians have talked endlessly about foreign victims such as George Floyd – an African American who died in Minnesota – they say almost nothing about the likes of

Rhiannon Whyte. Just as they have said virtually nothing about Charlene Downes, Lucy Lowe, Victoria Agoglia, and many other British women and girls who have been raped, trafficked, or killed by illegal migrants or Pakistani Muslim rape gangs.

While elites call the British people 'far-right' for talking about these issues, they have said very little about the eight-year-old girl in Lambeth allegedly raped by an asylum seeker from Pakistan; the ten-year-old girl in Stockport who was nearly kidnapped by an asylum seeker from Sudan; the twelve-year-old in Nuneaton allegedly kidnapped, strangled and raped by two asylum seekers; the twelve-year-old girl in Birmingham raped by an Syrian asylum seeker; the fourteen-year-old in Essex sexually assaulted by an illegal migrant from Ethiopia; the fifteen-year-old girl in Oxford raped by an Iranian asylum seeker as she left an under-eighteens disco; or the fifteen-year-old in Falkirk followed and raped by an Afghan asylum seeker. These are not isolated tragedies. They are the human face of a system in which suicidal empathy places outsiders ahead of the safety of British citizens.

Ask yourself: would countries such as China, Saudi Arabia or Japan tolerate this? No. Only Britain's elites are this deranged, in love with their own self-image and blind to the enormous costs that are paid by others.

Ten months after Rhiannon Whyte's murder, more than a hundred left-wing politicians, celebrities and campaigners signed an open letter in *The Guardian* insisting that illegal migrants pose no greater threat to women and girls than anyone else.

The letter, organised by the left-wing Stand Up to Racism group – signed by Shami Chakrabarti, Diane Abbott, Zarah

Sultana, Charlotte Church and Paloma Faith, among others –
made sure to identify the real problem. It is not broken borders
and importing people from cultures that treat women like second-
class citizens. It is, they said, 'the far right's racist lies'.

They said nothing about the cases just listed. They said
nothing about Dame Louise Casey's revelation that asylum
seekers and foreign nationals are involved in 'a significant proportion' of twelve live police investigations into rape gangs. They
said nothing about Ministry of Justice data showing foreign
nationals are more than twice as likely as British nationals to be
responsible for sexual assaults – with offenders from India,
Romania, Poland, Pakistan, Afghanistan, Nigeria, Sudan and
Bangladesh the most prolific.[16]

No amount of evidence will ever convince people who have
been radicalised into suicidal empathy. They are no longer interested in reality. All they are interested in is protecting a belief
system that makes them feel virtuous while others pay the price.

A SYSTEM DESIGNED TO FAIL

Illegal migrants who make it to Britain know the truth: once
here, they are very unlikely to be removed. The system is not
failing; it is built to fail. Most asylum claims are approved by
civil servants, who then point to these high approval rates as
proof that those arriving are 'genuine' refugees and the system
is 'working', ignoring the obvious fact that this encourages even
more people to come.

More than 108,000 asylum claims were filed in 2024, a record high. Nearly half were from people who had come on legal visas and then suddenly 'discovered' they were in need of asylum, often when they realised they would soon have to leave the country.

Of the almost 200,000 migrants who crossed the Channel illegally between 2018 and 2025, just 3.5% were deported by the state, with most of those returning voluntarily. If they were not Albanian and subjected to a specific return agreement between the UK and Albania, then their chance of being removed from Britain was less than 1%, revealing just how incompetent and ineffective the state has become in the face of this mounting crisis.

No wonder they keep coming. Britain might as well hang a big, flashing neon sign on the White Cliffs of Dover: 'If you make it here, you can stay'.

It is not just incompetence. It is a deliberate architecture of disorder built by a ruling class that sees the nation as a sinful relic, and illegal migrants as a source of moral redemption.

The financial costs are astronomical. Once again, they fall not on the elites who are presiding over this chaos but on the people who are now forced to live with it. The British people now have to pay roughly £15.3 billion in the coming years on housing asylum seekers and illegal migrants, enough to pay the annual salaries of 320,000 nurses.

Even more sickeningly, private companies gorge on this crisis, at the further expense of the British people. In 2025, it emerged that the companies Serco, Clearsprings Ready Homes and Mears had made £383 million in profits from asylum accommodation contracts that had been backed up by the British people's money. They offer landlords guaranteed five-year rental agreements, no management fees, free maintenance and all utilities and council tax paid for, using British taxpayers' money to outbid British tenants in their own housing market.

Graham King, founder of Clearsprings – nicknamed the 'Asylum King' – has become a billionaire. Profits for his company jumped from £763,000 in 2020 to £117 million four years later. In 2023, Clearsprings took in £1.3 billion of revenue.

In fact, the British state is now splashing out so much cash on this crisis that even the Chinese Communist Party wanted in on the action. The amount of money sloshing around is so vast that even organisations linked to the Chinese Communist Party have bought into it, acquiring hotels that are block-booked for asylum seekers and earning tens of millions in rent paid by the Home Office – and therefore by the British taxpayer.

THE REWARDS OF FAILURE

The one government department meant to keep the British people safe is the same department writing these cheques. The Home Office is not just failing; it has, in many respects, become a stakeholder in failure.

Nick Timothy, a former Downing Street adviser, concluded in an investigation that the Home Office is not just incompetent but has embraced a 'culture of defeatism' on immigration.

Instead of fixing the border, civil servants waste hours on

left-wing identity politics seminars and 'listening circles' about their feelings. Record-keeping is 'woefully inadequate', forecasts 'fatally overoptimistic' and the department is 'not fit for purpose'. Yet senior officials still think it is acceptable to pocket significant bonuses for their 'performance'.

In 2025, astonishingly, it was reported that senior civil servants such as Sir Matthew Rycroft were paid nearly half a million pounds – far more than the Prime Minister – plus extra bonuses and perks for failing to secure the borders.

This is what suicidal empathy looks like in practice – a state that rewards officials who fail to protect its own people, because the system's deepest loyalty is no longer to the nation but to an internationalist moral code.

HUMAN RIGHTS FOR ALL?

Behind all this lies a deeply corrosive legal framework. The European Convention on Human Rights (ECHR), born of post-war liberal idealism, has become a straitjacket that Britain's political class refuses to take off.

In the name of displaying 'empathy' to others, the ruling class allowed our own laws, courts and borders to be subordinated by foreign ones, often with disastrous consequences.

Unlike the Old Elite, who were suspicious of attempts to transfer power and control to supra-national bodies, today's elites think very differently.

Symbolised by the likes of human rights lawyer Keir Starmer, they include left-wing lawyers, judges, campaigners, activists and politicians, for whom foreign courts and international human rights laws are the highest form of moral authority imaginable.

These international human rights are then used to allow dangerous criminals and unvetted migrants into our country and prevent their removal. This is why somebody like binman Wayne Broadhurst, who left his home in Uxbridge in 2025 to walk his dog, was stabbed to death by an Afghan migrant he did not know named Safi Dawood. Dawood had entered Britain illegally and been allowed to stay.

It is why restaurant owner Gurvinder Johal was stabbed through the heart in Derby, in 2025, as he queued at a bank to withdraw wages for his staff. He, too, had never met his murderer, an asylum seeker from Somalia named Haybe Nur, who was allowed to stay in Britain while he appealed a decision to deport him.

And it is why British pensioner Terence Carney, who in 2023 left his home in Hartlepool for his usual morning walk, was murdered. Like the other victims, Carney had never met his murderer, an asylum seeker from Morocco named Ahmed Alid who later tried to justify his actions by pointing to the ongoing conflict in Gaza.

All three of these British men, alongside many more like them, were the victims of a regime that now routinely puts the interests and rights of outsiders ahead of its own people.

It all started with such high-minded intentions. After the atrocities of the Second World War, the Council of Europe was formed to promote democracy, human rights, and the rule of law.

The ECHR then entered into force in 1953. Even then, British leaders such as Winston Churchill only supported it on the assumption it would not undermine Britain's sovereignty.

Over time, however, the ECHR, morphed into a 'living instrument', interpreted ever more expansively and influencing more issues. Articles that appear reasonable in theory have produced extraordinary consequences in reality.

Article 3 ('No one shall be subjected to torture or inhuman or degrading treatment') and Article 8 (the 'Right to respect for private and family life') are now routinely used to block the deportation of foreign criminals, including sex offenders and terrorists.

In 2025, a Nigerian woman who had made eight failed attempts to claim asylum in Britain was finally granted the right to remain because she had joined a group – the Indigenous People of Biafra – that her own government considers a terrorist organisation. The judge accepted that she had joined cynically to bolster her claim but still allowed her to stay.

Article 3 is partly why it took nearly a decade to deport hook-handed hate preacher Abu Hamza to America, whose lawyers argued that conditions in a 'supermax' prison would breach his human rights.

It was also central to the decision to allow Afghan sex offender Abdul Ezedi to stay in Britain. Ezedi had arrived illegally in 2018, was later convicted of sexual assault and indecent exposure, then claimed asylum by pretending to convert to Christianity, arguing he would be persecuted if he was returned to Afghanistan.

A Baptist preacher vouched for him. The courts agreed. Those who knew Ezedi said he remained a practising Muslim and planned to travel to Afghanistan to find a wife. Instead, he threw acid over a woman and her three-year-old daughter in Clapham, south London.

Even if someone should not be in Britain, the ECHR, enshrined into UK law by Tony Blair's Human Rights Act, makes it extremely difficult to remove them from the country. Article 8 has been invoked time and again by a disgraceful catalogue of drug dealers and violent criminals who claim deportation would breach their 'right to a family life'.

In 2025, an Albanian drug dealer who arrived in Britain illegally and was jailed for running a cannabis factory was allowed to stay because deporting him would deprive his daughter of a 'male role model'.

Another man, from the Democratic Republic of Congo, was told he could remain in Scotland despite sexually assaulting his stepdaughter and two other young girls.

In 2025, the British people witnessed another almost unbelievable spectacle: their country being held to ransom by a convicted sex offender. Hadush Kebatu, an Ethiopian illegal migrant, arrived on a small boat, sexually assaulted a fourteen-year-old girl and another woman in Essex, triggered mass protests outside the taxpayer-funded Bell Hotel, and then vanished after being accidentally released from custody.

When officials finally prepared to deport him, he demanded £500 compensation and threatened a last-minute legal challenge if he was not paid. The money was handed over. How was this possible? Because the ECHR and the army of activist lawyers it empowers make this possible. Power has shifted away from the British people towards foreign courts and lawyers who have little interest in prioritising the nation-state.

And what of the rights of British citizens not to be forced to live alongside people who have broken their laws and pose clear risks to their safety?

That question never troubles the ruling class. In their moral universe, the rights of outsiders always come first – no matter what they do.

WHAT MUST BE DONE

In 2025, having finally grasped how serious the situation had become – or at least how serious it looked to the British people – the Labour government muttered about curbing the use of Articles 3 and 8. It will not happen. Reforming the ECHR requires international agreement and there is no appetite in Labour's ranks for loosening the legal regime they helped create.

Keir Starmer once wrote that human rights laws represent 'a new way of thinking' and we should see every decision through that prism. He meant it. The result is what we see today: a Human Rights machine that has turned British citizens into strangers under their own laws.

The Human Rights racket is the New Elite's thirty-year project. They cannot fix this crisis because they are its chief architects. Their 'solutions' are a form of moral theatre: designed to look serious while ensuring nothing changes. No matter the human cost, so long as they get to feel good about themselves that is all that matters.

Labour's behaviour since returning to power in 2024 proves

the point. It rushed to decriminalise illegal migration and scrap the Conservative Party's scheme to send illegal arrivals to Rwanda. That scheme was far from perfect, and as long as UK law is subordinated to European law it was always vulnerable to appeals, but it at least recognised the need for a strong deterrent that would discourage people from entering Britain illegally.

In its place, Labour unveiled the most absurd immigration policy in British history: a 'one-in, one-out' deal with France, trading small-boat migrants for asylum seekers with ties in the UK. Unsurprisingly, it was not long before deported migrants simply climbed on to new boats and came straight back, turning Britain's border into a farce. Labour has turned our border security into a game of Whac-A-Mole and left the British people even more at risk.

So, what must be done? I will answer this question more fully in the final chapter but some first steps are obvious. If Britain is serious about restoring control of its borders and protecting its own people then it must break with the entire framework that has produced the illegal migration crisis. It must leave the European Convention on Human Rights entirely, not tinker at the edges, and reject the jurisdiction of its court. It must also repeal Tony Blair's Human Rights Act, which hard-wired this system into UK law.

We cannot control our borders until we fully control our own laws. We must also detain and swiftly deport anyone who arrives illegally, processing their claims offshore, far from the communities that have already borne the greatest burden. Above all, we must also overturn the ruling class and its culture of suicidal empathy – the ideology that demands Britain sacrifice its own people to feel morally superior.

But before exploring in more detail how we might fix the country we must examine another way in which this ruling class is undermining our nation from within. It is not only presiding over mass uncontrolled immigration and broken borders; it is also turning the entire system against its own people through a policy of two-tier multiculturalism.

CHAPTER FIVE

TWO-TIER MULTICULTURALISM

Two events in 2025 capture almost perfectly the assault that is now being carried out on Britain's identity, culture and majority group.

In Warwickshire, a twelve-year-old girl named Courtney Wright wore a Union Jack dress for her school's 'Culture Celebration Day'. For this harmless act of pride in her country, her teachers pulled her aside and sent her home.

At the very same moment, across Britain's towns and villages, ordinary people suddenly began raising Union and St George's flags on public buildings and lampposts. But local councils – including many of the same councils that had been happy to fly Palestinian or Pride flags – rushed to tear the flags down.

To many elites in Westminster, Oxford and Cambridge these events meant nothing. But to millions of ordinary people they meant everything. They revealed, in one sharp moment, a truth that has been building for years: the ruling class no longer believes that the British majority should be allowed to express pride in their identity, their culture and way of life.

Courtney's school had encouraged pupils to 'proudly represent their heritage'. Yet when she represented the heritage of the majority, she was punished. She had even prepared a small speech about the importance of British culture, describing Britain's identity as 'modern, diverse and always changing'. It was exactly the sort of thing Westminster gatekeepers are supposed to applaud – except that it came from a child of the majority.

Her speech even contained an uncomfortable truth: 'It can feel like being British doesn't count as a culture, just because it's the majority.' Even at twelve, Courtney understood one of the unwritten rules of Britain's new hierarchy of identity.

She was not alone. Another child from a farming family was reportedly sent home for wearing a flat cap and checked shirt, symbols of a heritage the school had no interest in celebrating. The message could not have been clearer: every identity matters, except the identity of the majority.

Meanwhile, an entirely ordinary display of patriotism – the flying of the flag – was treated by elites as a dangerous eruption of extremism. Like many on the left, Labour MP Clive Lewis labelled those flying England's flag 'far right'. The academic Kehinde Andrews went on television to claim that the St George's Cross was a 'clear symbol of racism', adding it was 'no accident' these were the flags 'used on slave ships'. Football pundit Gary Neville joined in, criticising 'angry middle-aged white men'.

It did not stop there. Labour Prime Minister Keir Starmer declared an urgent need to 'reclaim the flag' from so-called 'toxic' and 'far right' people who were 'stoking division'. Countless others warned that flying the flag 'might make minorities feel uncomfortable'.

Councils across London, Manchester, York, Birmingham and beyond – which often took months to clear rubbish or fill potholes – suddenly acted with stunning speed to strip the flags from public view. In Malmsbury, Wiltshire, one man resorted to painting a St George's Cross over potholes simply to force his council to take notice.

Once again, the people saw things very differently from the New Elite. One survey by pollsters More in Common found nearly 60% of British people wanted to see the flags flown *more often* on buildings. They are not offended by their identity. Only the ruling class is.

How did we reach the point where a country treats its own majority as a problem? The answer lies in what I call 'two-tier multiculturalism' – a new doctrine among the ruling class that insists every identity must be celebrated and asserted except the identity of the majority.

It is the cultural side of the same suicidal empathy that has delivered mass immigration and opened Britain's borders without limit. It teaches elites that moral goodness is proven not by loyalty to their own people but by siding with outsiders, even at the expense of the nation they are supposed to serve.

Under this two-tier system, minorities are urged to retain their identities, languages and traditions, and take pride in who they are. But the majority is expected to shed its identity, apologise for its history, and redefine itself not around who *we* are but around who *others* are.

In this way, Britishness and Englishness are hollowed out.

They are reduced to empty placeholders for multiculturalism: identities you are allowed to express but only if you pretend they are no longer identities at all. This is how the identity of the majority is dismantled.

Britishness and Englishness are either redefined as a celebration of global 'diversity' – meaning other people's cultures – or recast as a source of shame and embarrassment. The majority must only exist to promote diversity in all its forms, to celebrate 'the Other' and focus on preserving the identities of every group except its own.

Yet the problem with this is immediately obvious to everybody outside the ruling class. To say that a nation is welcoming of outsiders is fine. But as the well-known academic Francis Fukuyama has pointed out, this cannot be the basis of a nation's identity because it is the same thing as saying that a nation has no real identity of its own.[17] If the only thing that defines a people is they welcome others then who are they, really? They don't exist, which is the point.

Minorities, in sharp contrast, *are* strongly encouraged to retain their own identities without having to make any such compromises or concessions. Hence the 'two-tier' nature of multiculturalism in Britain today: there is one rule for the majority, another for minorities.

This is no accident. It is deliberate and it is tearing our country apart. While mass immigration and porous borders fast-track the demographic replacement of the majority, minority groups are simultaneously urged not to integrate and remain separate.

Leaders show little interest in ensuring that newcomers speak our national language, embrace our national identity, adopt our way of life and are taught a balanced view of our history. In elite circles, even the word 'assimilation' has been recast as 'exclusionary' or 'racist'. They see no problem in the fact, as we saw in the previous chapters, that millions of new-comers in Britain refuse to share our identity or speak our language. Elites just shrug.

Meanwhile, people from the majority are constantly bom-barded with the message that their culture is illegitimate, their ancestors were 'racist', their history is shameful, and their very existence is an obstacle to 'progress'.

The result is deep division, resentment and a growing sense among millions that their home is being dismantled while they are told to applaud their own demise.

Two-tier multiculturalism, in other words, accelerates the demographic changes that are already underway. It hollows out the national culture that once made Britain coherent. And it leaves us with a patchwork of competing identities with no shared core to hold them together.

All this points in one direction: the loss of our country's distinc-tive character, its unique culture and identity and its sense of collective memory. Many ordinary people have begun to resist this. They are the Courtneys of Britain – the people who simply want permission to say they are proud of who they are. They are the men and women who raise their flag not as an act of hatred but as an act of belonging, and, increasingly, an act of resistance.

But their own governing class treats them as intruders in their own home.

THE ASSAULT ON BRITISHNESS

Why has British culture been singled out for erasure? What is so objectionable about our history and traditions that they must be dismantled?

Britain once believed in things that were sensible, even admirable: individual liberty, the rule of law, free speech, equality under the law, scepticism towards state power, a strong sense of duty and a deep belief in fair play and tolerance.

C. S. Lewis added to this list 'a love for the way of life; for beer and tea and open fires, trains with compartments in them and an unarmed police force and all the rest of it; for the local dialect and for our native language'. It was not an aggressive nationalism. It was loyalty, a shared affection for home. Yet today, these attachments are seen by many people in the ruling class as backward, embarrassing, even dangerous.

Why? Because over the last half-century, a powerful worldview took root in Britain's elite institutions – in schools, universities, the civil service, the BBC, museums, galleries, NGOs and corporate Human Resources departments.

Thinkers such as Sir Roger Scruton, Daniel Bell, Christopher Lasch and Professor Eric Kaufmann all warned about this mindset: what Bell called the 'adversary culture' of intellectual elites whose instinct is to reject Western civilisation while enjoying the benefits it produced.

What this later morphed into – Scruton pointed out – was a 'culture of repudiation' among elites in the institutions, a worldview that teaches citizens and especially young people to repudiate who they are by fixating on only the sins of their nation while ignoring its virtues.

By constantly attacking British culture, history and identity, by reframing these things as a source of shame and embarrassment, the people are left, as Scruton put it, with an overwhelming feeling of 'bewilderment and the loss of any sense of identity'. They no longer really know who they are.

Put yourself in the shoes of the New Elite. Once you believe the majority is guilty, racist and tainted, it becomes much easier for you to justify extreme policies like opening the borders or inviting in millions of migrants from elsewhere.

If your guiding belief is that moral worth in society is proved by siding with outsiders against your own people then the policies of opening the floodgates to millions of outsiders while denigrating your own people are entirely logical.

The result of this two-tier approach can be seen all around us. It can be seen in how the British state promotes Scottish, Welsh, Irish and minority identities as positive and morally worthy, while presenting English identity as 'racist', 'xenophobic' and something that should be closely monitored, managed or pathologised.

It can be seen in how any criticism of this state policy of two-tier multiculturalism has been aggressively shut down while the policy has been imposed on local areas regardless. In Bradford, in 1984, schoolteacher Ray Honeyford, became one of the first to be publicly ostracised and denounced as 'racist' for merely suggesting that Britain's schools should prioritise integration – including a shared English language and civic values.

Based on Honeyford's extensive experience and what he was witnessing among children in the classroom, he warned that multicultural policies were ghettoising Asian children and undermining the performance of White working-class children.

At the very same time, Bradford Council was pushing a strong form of two-tier multiculturalism which would eventually lead to the balkanisation of large parts of the city.

In 2001, a report by Lord Ouseley drew the same conclusion as Honeyford had reached nearly twenty years earlier, before he was widely criticised and kicked out of national life: Bradford had become strongly divided along racial, ethnic and religious lines, with highly segregated schooling and little integration.

There was also widespread public fear of crime and violence by 'untouchable' Asian gangs which West Yorkshire Police refused to tackle because they worried about being called 'racist' – an early, lethal example of suicidal empathy, where the authorities chose to protect their own moral reputation rather than protect their own people.

The same two-tier logic was reflected in how the anti-Black racist murder of Stephen Lawrence, killed by a gang of White men in 1993, quite rightly dominated the national debate and led to systemic changes in law and policing. Yet the anti-White murder of fifteen-year-old Richard Everitt the following year, in 1994, allegedly stabbed to death by Asian boys in Somers Town, north London, was completely ignored by the elite class.

More recently, the same approach can be seen in how the Metropolitan Police were discouraged from using stop-and-search to deter people carrying knives, on the grounds it is 'racist' toward Black communities, putting ideology ahead of the safety of Londoners.

In 2025, too, the Sentencing Council, inspired by Labour MP David Lammy, tried to embed a two-tier justice system into UK law – with minorities given more lenient sentences than people from the White British majority – until a strong public backlash forced them to retreat. Nonetheless, the instinctive impulse of the elite class was clear for all to see.

Meanwhile, problems that affect the majority – such as the persistent underachievement of White British working-class boys at every level of the education system – barely register as a concern. The New Elite are much more interested in debating how to get children from minority backgrounds into Oxbridge – even if it means lowering standards – than how to help White British children who are often the most left behind and disadvantaged in the country.

To police this policy of two-tier multiculturalism, an entire industry has sprung up to reframe the symbols of British identity as 'racist' and accuse anyone who dissents of the same. Just look at what has been denounced as 'racist', 'White supremacist', or 'colonial legacies', all of which reflect this ongoing effort to discredit the identity and culture of the majority.

To name just a few: the English countryside, cricket, geology, 'being nice' to others, rolling your eyes, dogs, *Alice in Wonderland*, the Royal Family, Queen Elizabeth II, among many more. Each case is just as absurd as the next, but the effect is not. This is how the New Elite justify the radical demographic experiment that I described in previous chapters.

By constantly pathologising the majority, they can reassure themselves that flooding the country with mass immigration is not reckless but morally required and righteous. As Professor Eric

Kaufmann puts it, the state policy of multiculturalism gradually evolved into a system that 'burdens the white majority with different obligations than ethnic minorities'.

Once you believe this, that there is something fundamentally wrong with the White British majority, then everything else follows. You can justify opening the borders to millions of outsiders. You can justify dismantling national identities. You can justify shaming the majority for wanting what every people in history has wanted: continuity, belonging, the familiar over the unknown, and a future for their group.

This moral framework is the essence of suicidal empathy. Borders are seen as an inconvenience at best, a moral crime at worst. Loyalty to one's own people is considered shameful. The majority now exists only to celebrate 'the Other'. And if its only purpose is to applaud the arrival of outsiders, then there is no reason why it should remain a majority at all.

This relentless cultural attack on the majority weakens its sense of identity, collective memory and esteem from within. It further erodes the nation and sets the stage for its demise.

The ruling class wants you to believe there is nothing particularly distinctive or special about being British or English; that the only thing binding us together is our enthusiasm for people who are not from here. But, then, who are we? As the American scholar Samuel P. Huntington warned, a nation must know who it is before it can know what its interests are.

Two-tier multiculturalism and mass immigration are not separate errors. They are two sides of the same project of national self-negation. One dissolves the borders; the other dissolves the identity those borders were meant to protect.

And this ideology now has consequences – real, measurable, often disastrous consequences – for social cohesion, trust and security.

THE MYTH OF INTEGRATION

According to the ruling class, Britain has nothing to fear from mass immigration because 'integration is working'. Diversity is making us stronger. Multiculturalism is a strength.

When making this case, they routinely point to passports and bureaucracy. They insist that anybody becomes British the moment they set foot on the country's soil and their papers are stamped.

But as many people know, belonging requires more than a piece of paper. It requires a deep emotional bond to the nation and its people. Yet as we have seen in recent years, the ruling class has allowed many people into our country who simply do not feel this bond.

Take Axel Rudakubana, the son of Rwandan immigrants who was described in media as a 'boy from Cardiff'. In July 2024, Rudakubana carried out a brutal attack on a children's dance class in Southport, murdering three helpless girls: six-year-old Bebe King, seven-year-old Elsie Dot Stancombe and nine-year-old Alice da Silva Aguiar.

Rudakubana may have been born in Cardiff – to parents from Rwanda – but nothing about his beliefs, attitudes, or emotional loyalties reflected British values.

He had tried to stab another pupil at school. He fantasised

about massacres. He stewed in grievance. After his arrest, he told police: 'It's a good thing those children are dead. I'm so glad. I'm so happy.' Yet the ruling class insisted he was as 'British' as the little girls he had murdered. He was not.

Nor was he an exception. Almost every major terrorist in Britain in the last twenty years or so has been a first- or second-generation immigrant. The 7/7 bombers, the killers of soldier Lee Rigby in 2013, the Westminster and London Bridge attackers, the Manchester Arena bomber, the murderer of David Amess – many were born here. Their parents were invited here.

But their children did not integrate. Why would they? They were raised in a culture where assimilation is now condemned as 'racist', where everybody is encouraged to see the White British as a threatening oppressor and where two-tier multiculturalism tells them that loyalty to Britain is optional while loyalty to grievance is rewarded.

The New Elite not only invited them in; they encouraged minorities to cling to their origin cultures, did not require them to integrate in any meaningful sense and changed the rules and debate around citizenship so that any criticism of this failure to integrate into the country was considered taboo and off limits. Suicidal empathy meant once they had opened the borders, they were now duty-bound to pretend everything was fine and to condemn as 'racist' anybody who said it was not.

Just look at the last thirty years in British politics. Every single commentator who has dared to suggest that this deeply flawed policy of multiculturalism is failing – from Suella Braverman to Trevor Phillips, Ted Cantle to Nigel Farage – has been roundly attacked.

When I pointed out the obvious truth in 2025 – that extremists such as Axel Rudakubana and the Islamist terrorists who blew apart their fellow citizens are not meaningfully British – I was denounced in *The Guardian* as 'far right' and 'racist'.

Because in the world of the New Elite, the 7/7 bombers are just as 'British' as the fifty-two people they murdered on that tragic day in 2005, while Salman Abedi, the 'British' citizen of Libyan descent, is just as British as the twenty-two people he murdered and the 250 he injured at an Ariana Grande pop concert at Manchester Arena in 2017.

But citizenship is not the same as belonging, and belonging requires more than a passport. It is an emotional allegiance. It is a strong bond. It is a deeper sense of 'us'.

A nation is a moral community, held together by a shared memory, culture and obligation. Many minorities who live in Britain and have integrated feel this strongly. But many others – especially those radicalised by Islamist ideology or raised within grievance-based tribal networks – do not. They feel only contempt for this country.

They do not feel what Scruton called 'oikophilia' – the love of home. This is the desire to become part of our shared inheritance, to feel that deeper bond to the country and a loyalty to the nation that transcends other loyalties.

What they feel instead is 'oikophobia' – a hatred for the very country and civilisation that has given them refuge. They refuse to integrate. They refuse to assimilate. They do not feel any emotional attachment to who we are. On the contrary, they despise everything about us. By murdering our own people, by declaring war on our country, they are openly showing us their primary loyalty lies elsewhere – and not with us.

They might be administratively British, but they are not one of us in a true sense. They have chosen to remove themselves from our community and our shared life. They do not belong because they do not want to belong. And yet our ruling class, consumed by suicidal empathy, tell us that to say this is somehow 'racist' or unacceptable. But it is not. It is reality.

MUSLIM SECTARIANISM

The dire effects of this two-tier multiculturalism cannot only be seen in how the ruling class has imported people who hate our way of life and refuse to integrate. It can also be seen in the rise of a dangerous new sectarianism in our politics.

Between 2001 and 2021, the Muslim population in Britain increased sharply from 1.6 million to 4 million – a 150% increase – and that excludes an estimated one million illegal migrants, many of them Muslim, and the vast Boriswave, which we explored in Chapter 3.

Some Muslims have integrated successfully into our national way of life. But it is also true that many have not. As I have already noted, in many areas of the country – Birmingham, Blackburn, Bradford, London, Manchester, Oldham – there are highly segregated Muslim enclaves where the White British are almost completely absent and Muslims have little meaningful interaction with the non-Muslim majority.

Into this vacuum has rushed a new dogma of radical identity politics and, in some places, hard-edged Islamist politics. We cannot ignore what this means.

Surveys have found alarming views among Muslim communities in Britain. Forty per cent of Muslims support gender-segregated education. Nearly half think that schools should insist on girls wearing the hijab or niqab. Nearly half of Muslim men think wives must obey their husbands. Nearly 40% think it is acceptable for a British Muslim to have more than one wife. The same share would support the rise of a 'Muslim-only' political party in British politics. A third want Sharia law implemented within two decades.[18] And nearly half of young Muslims want Islam declared Britain's national religion. These are not fringe numbers.

This is what happens when suicidal empathy meets mass immigration. First, you open the borders assuming everyone shares your values. Then, you construct a two-tier system at home that forbids the majority from defending their values while those who are invited in reject them.

We now see what this has enabled: sectarian voting blocs in British politics. Thanks to the failure of our leaders to slow the pace of immigration and assimilate newcomers, religious and tribal loyalties are now visibly transcending national ones.

Five independent MPs were elected on a pro-Gaza platform in 2024. A campaign group called The Muslim Vote boasts that Muslims can now determine the outcome in more than one hundred seats and demands new laws – like a definition of 'Islamophobia' that would shield Islam and cultural practices within Muslim communities from criticism.

Meanwhile, since 2024 some Muslim Labour MPs have

appeared to campaign more passionately for infrastructure in Pakistan – like a new airport in Mirpur – while opposing developments here in Britain, such as a third runway at Heathrow, on environmental grounds. Others have given speeches in the House of Commons appearing to defend blasphemy laws, cousin marriage, and suggest that concern about Muslim rape gangs was a far-right trope.

Inside prisons, meanwhile, Islamist gangs dominate entire wings. Muslims now form 18% of the prison population; in some jails, Islamist inmates and self-styled 'emirs' run the whole show, with officers relying on them to maintain order.

In 2024, masked Muslim groups marched through Birmingham, intimidating journalists and locals while police 'engaged with community leaders' instead of enforcing the rule of law on all groups, irrespective of their race or religion.

The next year, in 2025, Jewish football fans from Maccabi Tel Aviv football club were barred from attending a match in Birmingham on bogus public-order grounds, after a local Muslim politician met with West Midlands Police and local Islamists threatened violence.

Many people see hypocrisy. When conservative activists marched through the streets of London, in the same year, to voice their concerns about the state of the country, much of the political class went on media to denounce them as 'far right'.

But when independent Muslim MP Iqbal Mohamed was later filmed telling an all-Muslim audience, 'We must take over the whole of Birmingham, the whole of the West Midlands, the whole of the UK … we will not be taken for granted, and we will win', the political class barely stirred.

Clearly, there are many Muslims in Britain who do not share these views and would not condone these actions. But nor has there been much vocal opposition to them from within Britain's Muslim communities. Instead, as each year replaces the last, what we can see is more and more evidence of a worrying Muslim sectarianism taking root in British politics.

None of it is happening by chance. It is what happens when the ruling elite transplant radically different cultures into Western nations and then encourage minorities to stay separate from everyone else while shaming the majority for wanting to defend their own nation. This is the cost of two-tier multiculturalism. It is the cost of suicidal empathy.

AN UNFORGIVABLE BETRAYAL

The most horrifying consequence of this mindset – the clearest demonstration of what happens when elites choose moral vanity over moral duty – is the Pakistani Muslim rape gang scandal.

For decades, Pakistani Muslim networks groomed, raped, tortured, trafficked and terrorised vulnerable White working-class girls across Britain. Children, some as young as ten, were drugged, threatened, beaten, humiliated and passed from one abuser to the next.

They were lured with sweets and fizzy drinks and then plied with alcohol and drugs. They were threatened with violence against their families if they spoke out. Some were doused with petrol and threatened with being set alight. Girls begged for help.

They were ignored. Fathers were even arrested for trying to save their own daughters.

In years to come, people will ask: why did the leaders of a modern, supposedly civilised country like Britain allow the systematic rape and abuse of hundreds of thousands of its own children? Because the perpetrators – Pakistani Muslims – were from a minority group and the victims – White British working-class girls – were from the majority.

The rape gang scandal turned on its head the new moral code of the New Elite – the belief that all minorities are virtuous while the majority is bad.

It was the purest expression of two-tier multiculturalism: minorities must be protected at all costs, even if that means sacrificing the children of the majority. Elites were so terrified of being called 'racist' or 'Islamophobic' that they essentially allowed thousands of their country's own children to be raped, tortured and even killed.

The same suicidal empathy that drove our leaders to open the borders now made them terrified of defending their own children. Having built their careers on the claim that mass immigration is a moral triumph, they simply could not face the fact they had imported these barbaric attitudes and behaviours into Britain.

Authorities prioritised the need to avoid what they call 'community tensions' over their duty to safeguard children. They avoided prosecuting Pakistani offenders. They told whistle-blowers to be quiet. They lied. They covered it up. They betrayed the most vulnerable people.

The only reason journalists who did dare investigate the scandal – such as Andrew Norfolk at *The Times* – became so well known is because there were so few of them. For decades, the media class simply ignored the story altogether.

In early 2025, many journalists then attacked Elon Musk for highlighting the scandal and asking why there had been no national inquiry. It was ironic: the same media class that had consistently downplayed the scandal now attacked the one prominent person who was asking why it had been allowed to happen in the first place.

At every level, from the Home Office to local councils, there was a sustained effort to deny, downplay, deflect. It was an unforgivable betrayal. In Bradford, a social worker even attended the Islamic wedding of a vulnerable girl to her abuser and then arranged for her to be fostered by his parents, despite repeated reports of rape.

In Rotherham, a social worker who tried to raise concerns was told 'never, ever' to mention the ethnicity of the abusers again and was sent on a diversity training course. A police chief inspector told the father of a missing girl that the town 'would erupt' if it became known what was happening. A Labour councillor made a false allegation of 'racism' to shut down discussion of the scandal. He later resigned and took a role as a diversity manager in the NHS.

Across the country – in Telford, Oxford, Oldham, Sheffield, Peterborough, Birmingham, Leeds, and beyond – the story was the same: authorities failed White British children because they did not want to be called 'racist' or 'Islamophobic'.

In 2025, when independent MP Rupert Lowe raised the scandal again, former BBC journalist Emily Maitlis suggested he was 'probably racist' for doing so. The same year, when asked on the

BBC about the rape gangs, Labour MP Lucy Powell responded: 'Oh, we want to blow that little trumpet now, do we? Yeah, OK, let's get that dog whistle out.'

Incredibly, Powell is now deputy leader of the Labour Party. Weeks before, one of the independent 'pro-Gaza' MPs, Ayoub Khan, suggested the rape gang story was a 'false right-wing narrative'. Ask yourself: would politicians have made it this far if they had been seen to downplay the mass rape and sexual abuse of children from minority groups?

DEADLY HATRED

The attitudes of many rape gang perpetrators were explicit. They were driven by a hatred of the White British people and non-Muslims.

One girl in the North of England was raped more than a hundred times, called a 'white slag' and told she had to 'obey' or be beaten. Her main abuser quoted verses from the Qur'an while assaulting her.

In Oxford, Mohammed Karrar prepared a child for anal gang rape with a pump; at one point, she had 'four men inside her' and a red ball forced into her mouth. When she resisted, she was beaten with a baseball bat that was then inserted into her.

In Newcastle, a rapist shouted: 'All white women are good for one thing, for men like me to f*** and use as trash.' In Dewsbury, a victim was told: 'We're here to f*** all the white girls and f*** the Government.' In Rochdale, Shabir Ahmed ranted, 'we are the supreme race, not these white b******s'.

Many other victims testified that they were called 'white trash', 'white whores' and 'kaffirs'. They were preyed upon not despite their identity but *because* of it.

Again, none of this happened by chance. It is all a downstream effect of two-tier multiculturalism, of what happens when a ruling class transfers radically different and inferior cultures into their own while instructing its own people to not ask any difficult questions.

While everybody knows the name George Floyd, few know names like Charlene Downes, Lucy Lowe or Victoria Agoglia. Charlene Downes disappeared. Victoria Agoglia was injected with heroin and left to die. Lucy Lowe and her family were burned alive.

They were all murdered or 'disappeared' because the New Elite decided that the feelings of Pakistani men matter more than these children.

This is not a community cohesion issue. It is hatred. It is contempt. It is anti-White racism. It is violence born from a worldview that sees White working-class girls as subhuman and sees the majority as an enemy. It is not just that the ruling class did almost nothing to stop it. It is worse: they enabled it.

Two-tier multiculturalism has told elites they are virtuous when they repudiate their own heritage, indifferent when their own children are raped and courageous when they denounce the majority as racist. That is the true indictment.

THE PRICE OF SUICIDAL EMPATHY

Mass immigration and two-tier multiculturalism are not separate accidents. They are two parts of the same ideology, an ideology that demands Britain's borders be opened, its identity dismantled, the majority shamed and outsiders elevated.

It is an ideology that is now rapidly hollowing out the nation's ability to defend itself – morally, culturally and literally. For thirty years, Britain's elites congratulated themselves for their 'compassion' and 'empathy'. But it was not compassion. It was an abdication of responsibility. It was a refusal to defend their own people. It was suicidal empathy.

And the British people – patient, tolerant, slow to anger – have reached their limit. They know when they are being sacrificed. They know when they are being lied to. They know when their leaders no longer believe in the country they are supposed to serve. And they know what every people in history has known: a nation that cannot defend its borders, defend its culture, or defend its children is a nation that will not survive.

The three things that we have now examined – mass uncontrolled immigration, broken borders and two-tier multiculturalism – are why so many people in Britain now feel they are losing their country. But these things are not operating in a vacuum.

Today, they are being enforced and entrenched through something that we shall explore in the next chapter: a stifling regime of censorship and control.

CHAPTER SIX

CENSORSHIP INDUSTRIAL COMPLEX

If you want to replace a people, you need to silence them first. And if you want to neutralise any resistance, you will have to make sure that those who dare to speak out are severely punished, humiliated, blacklisted, or even imprisoned.

This is what is happening in Britain today, where the policies we have just examined – mass uncontrolled immigration, porous borders and two-tier multiculturalism – are being imposed alongside a regime of censorship that aims to shut down any opposition to them.

It was not always like this. Think of Britain today and then cast your mind back to the Britain of just a few decades ago. Those who are old enough to remember will not be able to avoid the sense that our country is now much less free than it used to be.

To those too young to remember, it can be hard to explain that it was not always like this. Today's young adults – younger millennials and zoomers from Gen Z – have known nothing except the straitjacket of political correctness, the language of 'diversity' and cancel culture. Many struggle even to grasp the idea of genuine freedom of expression. Some are not just sceptical that it is desirable; they fear and even hate the concept.

This mentality was shamefully exposed after the deadly shooting of American free-speech and conservative activist Charlie Kirk in Utah in 2025. Plenty of young people in Britain celebrated his cowardly murder on social media. Kirk, they said, had expressed 'hateful' views. Taking his life and depriving his children of their father was, they argued, fair game.

There it is in a nutshell: the tolerance of today's so-called 'progressives'. You have views I dislike, therefore you deserve to die. One attention-seeking British punk group, Bob Vylan, spoke for many young people when they said: 'If you chat s**t you will get banged. Rest in peace Charlie Kirk, you piece of s**t.'

Of course, it is not just the young who think like this. In recent years, after taking control of the institutions, the New Elite have succeeded in getting millions of Britons of all ages to accept a stifling regime of censorship – and even to volunteer to police it themselves.

In a sense, this attitude towards free speech is the most extraordinary achievement of our ruling class. They have made millions of people regard free speech not as a proud inheritance but with visceral hatred. And this in Britain, of all places: a nation whose tradition of freedom of expression was once admired across Europe and throughout the world.

THE DARK PATH

It was the Scottish philosopher David Hume, writing in the eighteenth century, who marvelled that 'nothing is more apt to surprise a foreigner than the extreme liberty which we enjoy in this country of communicating whatever we please to the public'.

But this was only ever a tradition, not something embedded in constitutional law. And within a few short years, these ancient liberties have been discarded. Fast-forward to today and British police now arrest more than thirty people a day for online posts they deem 'offensive'.

Why would the New Elite want to do this? Why wage war on the very freedoms that once defined Britain? The answer is simple: they have no choice.

The extreme policies they are now using to transform the country – through mass immigration, open borders and demographic change – are so deeply unpopular with the people they must adopt desperate measures to silence any opposition and discredit dissenters.

In earlier chapters we saw how suicidal empathy led the elite to open the borders and dismantle the majority. The other half of this story is censorship. If you are going to replace an entire people, you must first make it impossible for them to complain about it.

Mass immigration, broken borders and rapid demographic change have all been unpopular among the British people for decades. In 2025, as I was finishing this book, no less than two-thirds of British people told the reputable pollsters JL Partners that they support the immediate deportation of *all* illegal immigrants in the country. Only one in five, according to YouGov, think immigration is 'mostly good for the country'. And exactly one in three of all British adults said they were planning to vote for Nigel Farage and Reform UK, who have pledged to end mass uncontrolled immigration and regain control of Britain's borders.

The elite understands this perfectly well. They know the British people reject the transformation of their country, so they must ensure that these objections are never allowed to take political form. The elites can only proceed so long as what passes as our national 'debate' is tightly controlled, if not shut down completely. Suicidal empathy demands open borders; censorship ensures the population cannot resist the consequences that follow.

More than sixty years ago, US President Dwight D. Eisenhower warned his fellow Americans of what he called the 'military-industrial complex' – the unholy alliance between arms manufacturers and the armed forces that risked undermining democracy itself. Today, we live under a different but equally dangerous threat: what I call the Censorship Industrial Complex. This is the network of laws, institutions, ideologies and activists that is determined to crush dissent and brand any resistance to the ruling class as 'hate', 'extremism', 'terrorism', or 'misinformation'.

Just as the border regime exists to accelerate demographic change, the censorship regime exists to protect it. One dismantles the nation physically; the other dismantles it morally by stripping the people of their right to say they object. Together, they unravel the nation.

This is why today's Censorship Industrial Complex poses just as grave a danger to Britain's democracy as the military regime that Eisenhower feared.

Its rise began under New Labour, which devised measures such as the Human Rights Act, the Communications Act, the Equality Act and an array of so-called 'hate laws'. The Tories, for all their talk of free speech, did nothing to undo any of this during their fourteen years in power. In fact, they piled on further restrictions. The Online Safety Act, for instance, supposedly intended to protect children but in reality extended the reach of censorship even further, clamping down on what ordinary people can or cannot say online.

But the Censorship Industrial Complex is not just legislation. It is a culture among our ruling class – a set of behaviours and assumptions that stifle open and honest discussion. It is visible in our universities, in mainstream media, among pressure groups and charities, inside the police, and in almost any institution where power is wielded.

It uses the tools that I will show you in this chapter – policing language, inventing 'hate', de-platforming political opponents, expanding taboos, stretching concepts and redefining dissent as 'extremism'. All of these tools serve the same function: to protect the suicidal empathy of the elite from scrutiny and to insulate the demographic revolution that is reshaping the country from any democratic challenge.

In fact, this crisis is now so grave that we have even been warned about it by the president of the United States. Donald Trump has repeatedly voiced concern about the state of free speech in Britain. His vice-president JD Vance has also expressed alarm at the 'very dark path' Britain is going down while American free speech advocates like Elon Musk and journalist Tucker Carlson have added their voices to the growing clamour.

The attack on our free speech is very real, and we should be deeply worried by it, because free speech protects all the other liberties we cherish. As John Adams, one of America's Founding Fathers, warned: 'Liberty, once lost, is lost forever.' If we allow our free speech to be taken away, we will not get it back. And if we cannot speak freely about the project of demographic replacement then we cannot stop it.

AN END TO HATE

The rise of this Censorship Industrial Complex can be seen in the rampant spread of various 'hate laws' and the invention of things like 'non-crime hate incidents'. These measures are designed to control the boundaries of the debate, making it clear that questioning everything from mass migration to transgender ideology will no longer be tolerated.

Just think about those words for a moment: a 'non-crime hate incident'. This is straight out of a Soviet KGB playbook. The incidents are, by definition, not crimes. Yet they are recorded when a 'victim or any other person' decides that a 'protected characteristic', such as their race, gender, or religion, has been offended in some way.

Former police officer Harry Miller found this out in 2019 when he questioned on social media whether transgender women are in fact women. He was contacted by Humberside Police who told him they needed to 'check his thinking'.

In 2021, a non-crime hate incident was recorded when a man in Bedfordshire complained that his neighbour had whistled the tune to *Bob the Builder* at him. He claimed this was 'racial hatred'.

In 2018, an Asian man joked that his friend, who was also Asian and apparently found the joke amusing, looked like a terrorist. A third party reported this to the police, who duly recorded a non-crime hate incident.

This is not incompetence. It is conditioning. A population facing rapid demographic transformation must be trained to fear its own voice. The purpose of such surreal policing is not to stop 'hate', but to make ordinary citizens internalise the idea that speaking plainly about issues such as immigration, identity, or Islam is not just socially unacceptable, it is dangerous.

Since 2014, when non-crime hate incidents were introduced, an estimated 250,000 have been recorded by police forces in England and Wales, with one Westminster think tank estimating they consumed 60,000 hours of police time every year.

Unsurprisingly, in late 2025 even London's Metropolitan Police said it would no longer investigate non-crime hate incidents so that officers could 'focus on matters that meet the threshold for criminal investigations', with many other police forces promptly following suit.

But nobody should imagine that is the end of them. The mentality that created them is still firmly in place. A growing authoritarianism has taken hold among police. How else can you explain the case of Helen Jones, a grandmother in Stockport who wrote on Facebook in 2025 that a local Labour councillor should resign? Two plain-clothes police officers then knocked on her door to offer her 'advice'.

Or the case of Darren Brady, a former soldier who retweeted an image of a swastika made out of LGBT pride flags, during Pride Month in 2022? One of the Hampshire Police officers who visited his home told him: 'Someone has been caused anxiety based on your social media post. That is why you have been arrested.'

On Remembrance Sunday, in 2024, it was the turn of *Daily Telegraph* journalist Allison Pearson to be visited at her home by Essex Police officers, who told her she was being investigated for inciting racial hatred because of something she had posted on social media a year before.

Initially, the police had warned the newspaper against reporting they had visited, saying: 'it feels like an odd and potentially dangerous approach to take from the *Telegraph*'s side? I would very strongly urge you not to publish anything on this.'

It was never revealed to Pearson who had complained about her. Her tweet had included a photograph of Greater Manchester police officers posing with a flag of a Pakistani political party. She had incorrectly described the officers as being from the Metropolitan Police, and the flag as anti-Israel. A mistake, certainly – but a 'hate crime'? Really?

It is a striking indication of our political priorities that police spend their time pursuing law-abiding people, as they did with Graham Linehan, a writer and co-creator of the comedy *Father Ted*. In 2025, Linehan was met at Heathrow Airport by five armed officers from the Metropolitan Police, arrested on suspicion of inciting violence and later taken to hospital after his blood pressure spiked from the stress.

What had he done? He had made jokes online, including one about male-bodied trans women entering women-only spaces like changing rooms or toilets. He wrote: 'If a trans-identified male is in a female-only space, he is committing a violent, abusive act. Make a scene, call the cops and if all else fails, punch him in the balls.' J. K. Rowling, author of the *Harry Potter* books – who has herself been the subject of many attacks designed to silence her – responded to Linehan's arrest by saying that Britain is now a 'totalitarian' state.

Notice how the censorship always flows in one direction? It is aimed not at those who threaten the country's cohesion, but at those who defend it. This is what happens when you combine mass migration, a guilt-ridden elite and a policy of two-tier multiculturalism with a state that is increasingly determined to criminalise 'offence'. The result is a society in which the police and the state hunt thought crimes while turning a blind eye to real ones.

This is the same suicidal empathy that we saw in earlier chapters: a ruling class that views hostility towards the majority as understandable and loyalty to the majority as extremism.

THE LANGUAGE OF COMPASSION

The Censorship Industrial Complex relies on an entirely new vocabulary, a language that, superficially at least, appears to be built on compassion.

The New Elite restrict free speech in the name of ideas that sound entirely reasonable: supporting 'anti-racism', 'fighting hate' and 'protecting minorities'. But these slogans are not what they appear to be. They are not expressions of genuine compassion but, rather, cynical tools to shut down real discussion about what is happening in the country today.

I am by no means the first person to notice this. Sir Roger Scruton repeatedly pointed out how concepts such as inclusion and equality have morphed into powerful instruments of censorship and control. They are the real-life version of 'doublespeak', the concept derived from George Orwell's *Nineteen Eighty-Four*, his classic novel about a dystopian regime that controls every aspect of people's lives.

Doublespeak is what happens when the ruling class use language to disguise, distort and invert the meaning of words. It makes lies sound truthful and confuses people's attempts to understand reality.

In Orwell's novel the official slogans of the ruling regime are: 'War is peace. Freedom is slavery. Ignorance is strength.' These mantras are designed to make people give up on the idea of objective truth and to accept that whatever the regime says must be believed.

How does the ruling class today employ the same doublespeak? What is the vocabulary it uses to take control of taxpayer-funded institutions and private corporations?

'Diversity', for example, means celebrating every form of racial, ethnic, sexual and gender identity – except that of the majority. It manifestly never means diversity of thought, which is considered dangerous. Often the word diversity means its opposite: conformity.

'Inclusion' means including every perspective in society except that of straight White men, White majorities and people who hold conservative or gender-critical views that might clash with the worldview of the New Elite. Once again, inclusion becomes exclusion.

'Equality' means using the institutions of the state, and taxpayer-funded bodies, to engineer equal outcomes between different groups by openly discriminating against the White majority. That is not equality; it is a new form of prejudice.

'Anti-racism' means tackling racism against minorities through policies that discriminate against Whites. Again, it is the opposite of what it claims to be. In this way, as British writer Douglas Murray points out in his book *The Madness of Crowds*,[19] published in 2019, the ruling class, in the name of 'diversity', has built a regime that is not diverse at all.

It is a rigid new conformity, a tightly controlled groupthink, in which the people are no longer allowed to criticise, never mind challenge, the policies that are being imposed on them from above – from mass immigration to the demographic decline of the majority.

Every distortion of language serves the same deeper purpose: to make it impossible to describe the revolution taking place, and have a plain conversation about its implications.

A people who cannot name what is happening to their country cannot resist it. Suicidal empathy insists that the people must only welcome and celebrate everybody who comes to the country, while the new doublespeak ensures they cannot easily and clearly articulate the costs.

This is why language really matters and the language of confusion and deception has spread everywhere. You can see it in taxpayer-funded institutions such as the National Health Service issuing guidance about 'chestfeeding' rather than 'breastfeeding' so as not to offend trans people. Or hospitals avoiding the term 'vaginal birth' in favour of 'frontal or lower birth'. Or calling mothers 'birthing parents'. It explains the longstanding fear in the mainstream media of admitting that trans women have male anatomy – or even mentioning that only a tiny minority undergo genital surgery.

It is also the reason, we are told repeatedly, that there is no such thing as an 'illegal immigrant' – only 'undocumented' or 'irregular' migrants with 'insecure immigration status', even though the British people clearly know tens of thousands of migrants break our laws every year by entering the country illegally.

It is evident in the office of the Mayor of London, Sadiq Khan, telling employees they must not describe female genital mutilation or forced marriage as 'cultural practices'. Instead, Khan wants them to be called only 'harmful practices', even though they are cultural practices that only ever exist in particular minority communities. The reality is blurred to spare the feelings of some, even if that leaves others – girls and women – unprotected.

Meanwhile, the language used to describe anyone who disagrees with the ruling class is equally revealing. Opposing mass uncontrolled immigration is 'far right' or 'hate'. Wanting to control the borders is 'racist'. Speaking publicly about the rape gangs – including calling for a national inquiry – is, according to Prime Minister Keir Starmer, 'jumping on a far-right bandwagon'. Wanting to preserve your own culture and your own country is 'stoking the culture wars'. Voicing concern about the growing influence of Islam is 'Islamophobic'. Sharing your worry about the failure of integration or the pace of demographic change is 'xenophobic'.

In this way, the New Elite both ring-fence the project of replacement from criticism and discredit those who are trying to conserve their country by stopping this project from taking place to begin with.

What all this amounts to is what Professor Eric Kaufmann has called 'the diversity taboo' – an agreement among elites that issues such as mass immigration, demographic change and the status of White majorities in Western societies are no longer considered topics that can be openly discussed. They are being taken off the table, placed beyond the realm of legitimate politics, while those who dare talk about them are ostracised.

Suicidal empathy, in this linguistic form, insists that the feelings of outsiders must never be hurt, even if that means silencing insiders who are trying to warn that their country is being dismantled.

SPECIAL CASES

Defending free speech means defending the right of people to say things we may find deeply unpleasant, even disgusting. If free speech only protects polite, establishment-approved opinions, it is not free speech at all.

In 2024, following riots after three young girls were murdered in the town of Southport, childminder Lucy Connolly made a highly offensive and inflammatory social media post. 'Mass deportation now', she wrote, 'set fire to all the f*****g hotels full of the b*****ds for all I care. While you're at it take the treacherous government and politicians with them. I feel physically sick knowing what these families will now have to endure. If that makes me racist so be it.'

I do not for a second condone what she said, but did it deserve the thirty-one months in prison to which she was sentenced? This was a longer sentence than those given to some members of the Pakistani Muslim rape gangs.

Connolly deleted the post a few hours later. She then urged people not to join the unrest. She had no criminal record. She had a young daughter and a sick husband. Still: thirty-one months.

Your right to free speech in Britain today depends on who you are and whether your views align with those of the New Elite. If you are Livia Tossici-Bolt, a White retired medical scientist and anti-abortion campaigner, you are not very high up the hierarchy. In 2023, she was convicted of breaching an abortion clinic 'buffer zone' and ordered to pay £20,000 in costs for holding a sign outside a clinic in Bournemouth that read: 'Here to talk, if you want'.

Meanwhile, Isabel Vaughan-Spruce, a charity worker, fared even worse. Forget free speech: West Midlands police arrested Vaughan-Spruce on two occasions simply for praying – in silence – near an abortion clinic in Birmingham. She was told: 'You've said you're engaging in prayer, which is the offence.' She rightly responded that 'silent prayer cannot possibly be a crime – everyone has the right to freedom of thought'. She eventually won compensation. But compare her treatment to that of others guided by their religious belief.

Shortly after Hamas terrorists flooded across the Israeli border and killed 1,200 Jews in October 2023, a preacher at a mosque in Ilford, east London, gave a sermon calling for the destruction of the Jews. 'Oh Allah, curse the Jews and the children of Israel', he said. 'Oh Allah, curse the infidels and the polytheists' – by which he meant Christians. The police decided there was no case to answer.

Another preacher at a mosque in Northampton implored the Almighty to take vengeance on Jews. 'Kill them indiscriminately and do not leave any of them alive', he said. 'Make them captive to the Muslims.' Once again, the police took no action.

What such cases reflect is how, through the Censorship Industrial Complex, the New Elite have also moved to shut down debate about one of the most important issues of all: Islam.

After taking power in 2024, Keir Starmer's Labour government quickly pressed ahead with a sinister plan to impose a dogmatic new definition of 'Islamophobia' on Britain's institutions. This would make it difficult to criticise the conduct of any Muslims without risking a hate crime accusation.

An earlier version of the definition, put forward in 2018, by an All-Party Parliamentary Group and supported by Labour – including the current Home Secretary, Shabana Mahmood – gives a sense of what this is *really* about. It offers a fascinating and terrifying glimpse into the mindset of the New Elite.

Astonishingly, that definition suggested that merely talking about 'grooming gangs' – the Pakistani Muslim rape gangs – could be considered 'Islamophobic'. It described discussion of the rape gangs as a 'subtle form of anti-Muslim racism' and a 'modern-day iteration' of 'age-old stereotypes and tropes about Islam and Muslims'.

Its aim was precisely what led to the rape gang scandal being covered up in the first place: shutting down free speech so as not to 'offend' or 'emotionally harm' communities in which some Muslims had been raping non-Muslim children. This is classic suicidal empathy: eroding the free speech of the majority to avoid hurting the feelings of minorities.

One member of the working group, Baroness Shaista Gohir, even wrote a report expressing concern about the 'disproportionate media coverage of Asian offenders', which, she said, enabled 'right-wing populist groups' to 'fuel racism and Islamophobia'. In reality, the media went nowhere near far enough in reporting on the problem.

Nor was this all. The same definition suggested that talking about the demographic rise of Islam in a negative way could also be 'Islamophobic'. In other words, suggesting that the rapid growth of Islam in Western societies might have serious consequences for the rights of women, sexual minorities, or the separation of church and state, could become a 'hate crime'.

The definition would also have made it 'Islamophobic' to talk about 'Muslim entryism' in British politics – including, perhaps, blatant attempts by Islamic organisations and campaigners to infiltrate and influence public institutions. What, then, might we be allowed to say in future about campaign groups like The Muslim Vote, which is openly trying to organise millions of Muslims in Britain to vote along religious lines?

We are being pushed towards a dark, deeply Orwellian

world in which, if the New Elite have their way, the British people will be unable to criticise Islam, the cultural practices of Muslims, or the negative changes that are happening in our country because of these demographic trends. The key point is clear: if you cannot criticise a religion or demographic change, you cannot resist it.

THE BLASPHEMERS

Any such legislation to essentially outlaw 'Islamophobia' or 'anti-Muslim hostility' would amount to a law against blasphemy, making it all but impossible to criticise Islam, a status that must not be afforded to any religion in a civilised society.

Yet in 2025 Britain came within a hair's breadth of a blasphemy law by the back door, after a ruling in the courts. A Turkish-born man, Hamit Coskun, was found guilty of a public order offence after he burned a copy of the Qur'an outside the Turkish consulate in London, as part of a protest against that country's regime. He shouted 'F*** Islam' and said that it was a 'religion of terrorism'.

His actions were deemed to have disturbed the peace. In what way? Astonishingly, part of the evidence against him was that a Muslim onlooker had threatened to murder him. A man called Moussa Kadri shouted at Coskun, 'I'm going to kill you'. He then fetched a knife and slashed at his victim in a crazed attack.

Needless to say, the man wielding the knife, Kadri, was later given a suspended sentence, rather than jail time. The judge excused him on the grounds that he had clearly been 'deeply offended' by the burning of the 'holy Qur'an', and besides, the judge said, the knife 'was not that sharp anyway'. Coskun, the victim of the attack, was found guilty and fined. Thankfully, that decision was reversed on appeal four months later, but we came very close to setting a chilling precedent.

Our legal system almost approved making blasphemy, in effect, a crime. That would have been a truly dangerous evolution of the Censorship Industrial Complex, which is already out of control. It is not as if the problem of violent reactions to perceived insults to Islam is new. As long ago as 1989, around a thousand members of Bradford's Muslim community marched through the city to burn Salman Rushdie's novel *The Satanic Verses* on the grounds that it was blasphemous.

The Supreme Leader of Iran, Ayatollah Khomeini, urged all Muslims to kill Rushdie, along with anyone involved in publishing the book. Despite living in Britain, Rushdie was forced into hiding. A group of Muslim lawyers tried to get the book banned in the High Court.

In a real sense, that was the fork in the road. Our ruling class was faced with a choice: do we hold Islam to the same standard as every other faith, or do we capitulate and offer special treatment? They chose the latter, because they thought the most important thing was not to offend anyone.

Things have only deteriorated since. Consider what happened to a teacher at Batley Grammar School, in West Yorkshire, in 2021, who made the nearly fatal mistake of showing pupils a cartoon of the Prophet Muhammad. As part of a lesson about free speech, blasphemy and 'controversial topics', all of which is in the country's national curriculum, the religious studies teacher shared images of Muhammad, the Pope and Jesus Christ.

Soon afterwards, Muslims in Batley and surrounding areas began not just protesting but harassing the teacher and threatening his life. His name, picture, car, and home address – as well as those of his partner – were all shared online. Groups of Muslim men gathered outside his home. The teacher was forced to go into hiding, fearing for his life and those of his children.

This took place just six months after a French teacher, Samuel Paty, had been beheaded at the gates of his school for the 'crime' of showing a cartoon of Muhammad during a class on free speech.

How was this allowed to happen in Britain? The answer is found in an independent report published in 2024. It reveals how the teacher received virtually no support from West Yorkshire Police. The local council did not want to know. The local Labour MP, Tracy Brabin, quickly issued a statement, apologising not to the teacher whose life had been destroyed but for the 'offence caused' to the Muslim community.

Across institutions, the report concluded, there was – in a single sentence that symbolises the wider problem of suicidal empathy in Britain – 'a disproportionate concern for not causing offence to the religious sensibilities of those who … chose to engage in intimidation and harassment'. In other words, the authorities were far more interested in appeasing and encouraging radical Islamists than protecting the free speech and basic rights of a schoolteacher who had been forced into hiding.

Here again is the logic of suicidal empathy: the rights of the majority are negotiable, but the sensitivities of certain minorities are sacred. And when rapid demographic shifts create large, assertive blocs, the elite instinctively capitulates rather than defend its own civilisation.

Once again, the feelings of an aggressive minority were considered more important than the safety and freedom of their fellow citizens.

WE ARE ALL TERRORISTS NOW

It is ironic that the people who claim to be the most open and tolerant are often the most intolerant of those who hold different views. The ruling class reserves a special hatred for those who tell the truth about what is really going on.

Just look at the official government guidance, released in 2025, which makes clear that the British state now views anyone who holds culturally conservative views or is critical of immigration as somehow equivalent to a terrorist.

An official counter-terrorism Prevent training course, leaked to the press, stated that believing Western nations are under threat from mass immigration and a lack of integration by certain ethnic and cultural groups is a 'sub-category' of so-called 'extreme right-wing terrorist ideologies and their narratives'.

President Trump's warning, for instance, in 2025, that European nations like Britain are 'facing civilisational erasure' on account of the fact that 'within a few decades at the latest, certain NATO members will become majority non-European', would be considered to be associated with right-wing extremist terrorist ideology. In fact, in late 2025 a schoolteacher was even referred to Britain's counter-terrorism Prevent programme after showing his politics students videos of speeches by President Trump.

This is how the New Elite think. To support their cause is to be virtuous and morally righteous. To oppose it – to question whether it is wise to replace your own people and dismantle your own culture – is to be beyond the pale, akin to a terrorist.

This is why, inevitably, when this book is published, they will attack me, too. They will employ all the usual taboos and labels – 'far right', 'racist', 'extremist' – to try and discredit this work, as they try to discredit all heretics.

Meanwhile, what they will want to avoid is how, in 2025, a devastating dossier revealed the blatant bias at the heart of our state broadcaster, the BBC. It was written by former journalist Michael Prescott, who had been appointed as an independent adviser to the BBC's Editorial Guidelines and Standards Board.

The report disclosed how *Panorama* had doctored one of Donald Trump's speeches to make it appear he was calling for violence. It revealed how BBC Arabic's reporting on the war in Gaza devoted generous coverage to the views of Hamas and how a faction of LGBT reporters censored coverage of the trans debate. And it highlighted how Verify – the BBC's own fact-checking service – had produced a report falsely suggesting that car insurers were racist.

Prescott's warnings were ignored by BBC senior executives. They simply were not interested. When the report eventually came to light, the scandal ended with the resignation of the BBC's director-general, Tim Davie. But nobody should imagine this will deter the New Elite for long. Their determination to present the facts only as they see fit, and to marginalise dissenting voices, remains undiminished.

In our universities, where the New Elite are taught what to think, I have witnessed the same assault on free speech and diversity of thought.[20] Seats of learning that were once interested in truth and debate have morphed into closely policed, controlled echo chambers in which dissent is not permitted. Left-wing dominance is now an established fact.

Whereas seventy years ago there were around three left-wing scholars for every right-wing scholar, today the ratio is closer to ten to one. What, then, should we do, as a culture of silence is imposed upon us, step by step? How do we dismantle the Censorship Industrial Complex and reclaim the right to speak and voice dissent?

Our institutions will be difficult to recapture, but we can start with our laws. We must be free to offend others – indeed, to be 'grossly offensive', which Section 127 of the Communications Act makes a crime.

We must not allow our leaders to determine the truth on our behalf, as Section 179 of the Online Safety Act suggests they can, by making it an offence to spread 'disinformation'.

Above all, we must defend our free speech if we wish to continue living in a free society. Without it, we cannot defend our borders, our culture, or our people. Without it, we cannot even describe what is being done to us.

The alternative is truly grim. It is subjugation. A people stripped of their speech is a people prepared for replacement. A nation that cannot name what is happening to it cannot hope to stop it.

Suicidal empathy opened the gates. Two-tier multiculturalism told the majority they no longer have a culture worth defending. And now the Censorship Industrial Complex holds the line, punishing anyone who dares to resist.

A nation undergoing large-scale demographic transformation cannot remain democratic if its people are forbidden from discussing this process.

That is why censorship has become the enforcement arm of this demographic change: it prevents debate, neutralises resistance and ensures the majority stays silent as the country they built is now remade around them without their consent.

If we surrender our right to speak, we will have surrendered everything else. And if the people do not start to reclaim their voice, they will lose their country.

The stakes could not be higher.

CHAPTER SEVEN

LONDON HAS FALLEN

If you want to see the future that awaits Britain, you do not need a crystal ball or great gifts of imagination. You need only visit London. London is no longer just a city. It is living proof of what happens when elites in the grip of suicidal empathy take control.

Immigration without restraint. Two-tier multiculturalism. Muslim sectarianism. And – most visibly of all – the near-complete demographic replacement of the people who built the city, and indeed the country.

In London, all the poisons I have described in this book – porous borders, identity politics, elite self-hatred and a total disregard for the majority – have combined in one place. London is where the whole story comes together: broken borders supply the numbers, two-tier multiculturalism decides whose side the state is on and suicidal empathy provides the moral script that tells elites it is noble to preside over their own people's decline.

When it comes to the project of demographic replacement, London is simply streets ahead of Britain and shows what will happen nationally if we stay on our current course.

London's transformation has been staggering. Between 1961 and 2021, in less than a lifetime, the share of White British people collapsed from 95% to just 37%. Today, given the enormous levels of migration since the last census – including the Boriswave – it is likely that the White British make up *less than one-third* of people in the country's capital city.

Nothing like this has ever happened anywhere before in peacetime. The historic ethnic majority is now falling, and falling fast.

You can see the sheer pace of this change by looking at London's schools. In 2025, just 22% of children in London's schools were White British. They are now a minority in all thirty-two of London's boroughs apart from Bromley, where they make up only half.

In nurseries, the picture is even starker. The White British are a minority in nurseries across the capital. In Tower Hamlets, shockingly, they make up less than 9% of children, less than 6% in Ealing, less than 4% in Harrow. In places like Barking and Dagenham – once a stronghold of the White working-class that supported the local Ford factory – they make up only 14% of primary school pupils.

Their numbers have simply fallen off a cliff.

What does this scale of change look like in schools? At Townley Grammar School in Bexley, in south-east London, the White British share slumped from 70% in 2007 to 17% in 2023 – in less than twenty years. In Queensmead School in Hillingdon, west London, it fell from 71% to 22%.

Nor are these remarkable shifts the only visible sign of demographic replacement. In 2025, the Department for Education quietly revealed that in most of London's primary schools English is no longer the preferred language for most pupils.

The share of children whose main language is no longer English is staggering – 57% in Barking and Dagenham, 62% in Ealing, 66% in Brent, Harrow and Tower Hamlets, 72% in Newham. One in four of *all* Londoners, not only children, no longer speak English as their preferred language, while some 320,000 cannot speak it at all.

In London, the capital city that is supposed to reflect the nation, a shared language is already a thing of the past. A city that no longer shares a language and no longer has a clear majority is not just 'diverse'; it is being redefined on entirely new terms, without anyone having been asked to consent.

Like Britain, London is also being transformed in other ways. In the latest census, four in ten of the city's residents were born overseas. More than one in seven – roughly 1.5 million people – are Muslim. And all this was before the Boriswave swamped Britain, bringing more than four million migrants into the country, so these numbers will have risen.

Since Blair first opened the floodgates in 1997, London's population has surged from seven to nine million. But, of course, nobody really knows how many people live in our capital.

One recent estimate put the number of illegal migrants in London as high as one person in every thirteen. Many of the illegals crossing the English Channel head straight for the Big Smoke.

A SIGN OF WHAT IS TO COME

Why is all this worth getting worked up about? Because what is happening in London tells us much about what will soon happen in the rest of the country.

In 2025, I published my forecast that White British people will slide into minority status across Britain by the year 2063. David Goodhart, author of the highly influential book *The Road to Somewhere* (2017) expressed best why these projections made so many people feel so deeply anxious: 'I heard nobody saying, "rapid demographic change is nothing to worry about – just look at London",' he wrote in the *Evening Standard*.

He has a point. Many people in Britain look at London and think to themselves: *I hope the rest of the country doesn't go the same way.*

Why do they feel like that? For a start, many people recognise that London has utterly failed the historic majority in this country. White British working-class inhabitants have been pushed out by mass immigration and a ruling class that no longer cares about them.

The people can sense this did not happen by accident. It flowed from the very mentality we saw in earlier chapters: a ruling class that thinks compassion means opening the city to the world, no matter what that does to the people already here.

Then there is the economy. You will remember how the British people were told mass immigration would make us all better off. That turned out to be a lie. As we saw in Chapter 3, much of the migration that has flooded Britain has been a net drain.

In London, vast amounts of cheap, unskilled labour have not fuelled an economic miracle. Far from it. They have just added to an already severe cost-of-living crisis, which goes far beyond £8 pints of beer and £4 cups of coffee.

Rents have nearly doubled in the last fifteen years, while earnings have gone up by just one-fifth. Living independently in London on a low or even average wage is now essentially impossible. Young liberal professionals proclaim the city to be 'the best and most diverse city in the world' yet simultaneously cannot afford their own home. The average rent is now over £2,700 a month, more than three-quarters of take-home pay for a higher-rate taxpayer earning £55,000.

At the same time, competition for support from the state has never been fiercer – and once again it is often the native British who lose out. In almost half of all London's social housing, the head of the household was not even born in Britain, a point we will return to.

And because many high-earning French and German bankers have since been replaced by low-earning food-delivery drivers from outside Europe, many migrants in London now earn wages so low that they rely heavily on the state and the British taxpayer. Illegal immigrants often work for less than the minimum wage, so the 'Deliveroo economy' is running rampant.

All this strikes another blow to the British people's sense of fair play. Bit by bit, the social contract is falling apart. There is a palpable loss of trust. Crime is leaving Londoners in fear and driving away terrified tourists.

Meanwhile, Labour's multicultural dream has soured, with

many immigrant communities failing to integrate. What began as a project the elites sold in the language of 'tolerance' and 'empathy' has curdled into something much darker.

This is especially noticeable among London's more than 1.5 million Muslims, many of whom live in highly segregated ghettos and show little serious interest in integrating. While you will not hear much about this among the ruling class, who insist that London is a 'paradise of diversity', there are many Muslim enclaves in London which – as we will see – are giving rise to a new and dangerous sectarianism.

In the east of the city, Muslims already make up at least 40% of Tower Hamlets, 35% of Newham, 31% of Redbridge and about one-quarter of Barking and Dagenham. In recent years, in these areas and others, the rest of the country has been forced to watch endless pro-Palestine and pro-Hamas marches shut down parts of the capital, alongside sickening scenes of 'Londoners' celebrating the mass murder and rape of Jews in Israel, on 7 October 2023, a grim new reality that forced Metropolitan Police to step up patrols.

What this reflects is the argument made by Garett Jones, which I shared in earlier chapters: people who have often been in Britain for decades still retain the cultures of their nations of origin, transplanting these radically different cultures into our own. Many simply refuse to integrate and share our identity, values and way of life.

You can see this, for instance, in official statistics which show what is happening in some of London's neighbourhoods. Take Southall Green East, in Ealing. More than three-quarters of people living in social housing, paid for by the British people, were born outside Britain, and of whom only 43% are in work and contributing to the economy.

Not even one in three residents in this part of London were born in Britain. More than one-third live in households where no adults speak English. And the number who identify with a 'non-UK identity' is larger than the number who embrace our national identity.

Yet still elites insist these areas are as genuinely 'British' or 'English' as anywhere else in the country. In reality, they not only reflect how the social contract is breaking down; they have also become hotbeds for extremism and terrorism.

As we will see, the mindset of suicidal empathy is not only leading elites to import people who are weakening our society; they are also importing people who hate Britain and are destroying the country from within. Look at London and you will see the abject failure of the project that our ruling class, guided by this mindset, has forced upon its own people.

DEATH OF THE COCKNEY

If this scale of demographic replacement had occurred in a capital city anywhere else in the world it would have been met with amazement, shock and outrage. Can you imagine Delhi being emptied of Indians? Tokyo emptied of Japanese? Beijing emptied of the Chinese? Abuja emptied of Nigerians? And the ruling class of those nations celebrating that fact?

It is inconceivable. Yet this is exactly what has taken place in our capital. In the London boroughs of Westminster, Tower Hamlets, Redbridge, Hounslow, Harrow and Ealing, the White British share has already collapsed to below 30%. In Brent and Newham, it has fallen below 20%. In many neighbourhoods the White British are barely visible at all.

There are now parts of the capital – Ealing, Newham, Brent, Redbridge, Hounslow, Harrow – where they do not even make up 10% of the population. Next time you visit London take a stroll around areas like Southall Broadway (2% White British), Dormers Wells (4%) or Clementswood (5%). As the economist Paul Collier has remarked: 'I can think of no other capital city where the indigenous population has more than halved in half a century.'

There is zero sympathy among the New Elite for London's vanished inhabitants, the people who built the city – and the country – in the first place: the White working-class. No sympathy for those like Alec Penstone, born in Hackney in London's East End on St George's Day 1925. Today, at 100 years old, Penstone holds the title of Britain's oldest poppy seller.

When the Second World War broke out his family were living in Tottenham, and as soon as he was old enough he joined the Royal Navy as a sonar operator, serving on convoys to Russia and taking part in D-Day in 1944.

But it was only in 2025, as one of Britain's last surviving veterans, that he came to national prominence when, live on mainstream television, he expressed the view that the ultimate sacrifice his comrades had made during the war had not been worth it after all.

'Rows and rows of white stones – all the hundreds of my

friends and everybody else – and for what?' he asked. 'The country of today?'

Yes, the sacrifice had been worth it for the country that Britain once was, but not for the one it has become. 'I don't know what the hell we fought for,' he said. 'The country has gone to rack and ruin.'

Like so many other White British people born in London, Penstone later left the capital. Somehow, during his life, the rules of the game were changed, without anyone ever asking him. His home was gone for ever. And the world in which everyone understood there was a strong social contract – where people would go so far as to lay down their lives for each other – was gone as well.

Before we examine what London has become today, let us pause for a moment for the disappeared Londoners, for a community with its own distinct identity, culture, and even its own dialect.

Not so long ago, they were synonymous with the capital. London meant Cockneys. For hundreds of years Cockneys were defined as anyone born within the sound of the Bow Bells. In quieter times gone by, these bells could be heard up to five miles from the Church of St Mary-le-Bow on the eastern edge of the old city.

The word 'Cockney' had originally carried connotations of being pampered, but London's working class were anything but pampered. They endured Dickensian deprivation and squalor, toiled in the factories and on the docks of the East End and became the target of the Luftwaffe's onslaught during the Blitz.

There is a reason most famous Cockneys are getting on a bit, people like Michael Caine and Alan Sugar. Many, like Barbara Windsor and Bobby Moore, have already reached the pearly gates. There are very few young Cockneys.

That is because the Cockney community and identity have all but vanished from London. Look, for instance, at the share of White British people in areas that were traditional strongholds of the Cockneys – Aldgate (14%), Whitechapel (16%), Spitalfields (17%) and Bethnal Green (18%). Even these figures include professionals and gentrifiers who have moved in from elsewhere, not the old White working class.

How would you describe the disappearance of an entire people from their home within a single lifetime? I'll leave you to think about that one. Elites call it 'diversity'. To the people who have lived it, it feels much more like displacement – the human face of the demographic replacement that we have mapped out in this book.

THE HOUSING RACKET

The Cockneys did not simply decide to up and leave one day. They were pushed out by economic conditions and excluded from social housing.

While you will never hear this from the New Elite, who own their homes in affluent parts of the city, much of our scarce housing now goes to people who are not even British.

To get a sense of the scale of the problem consider this: in 2024, Keir Starmer and the Labour Party committed to building 1.5 million new homes, but more than half these homes will be needed just to keep up with the relentless demand that has been generated by *past* immigration – and before anybody else has migrated into Britain.

In 2023, Bloomberg reported that immigration has pushed up rents by around 7%. The think tank Capital Economics found that the number of rental households formed by new immigrants surged from 80,000 in the 2010s to 200,000 today, inflating rents.

In 2025, another think tank, Onward, likewise found that since 2001 immigration has increased private rents across Britain by £132 a month, and by £216 in London, pushing many homes beyond the reach of British people, though especially young people.

Clearly, mass immigration is not the only reason for Britain's acute housing crisis, but it is a big reason. You can either have immigration on the scale Britain's rulers are forcing on the country, or you can have more available and affordable housing. You cannot have both.

These pressures are especially visible in social housing. Roughly two-thirds of London's nearly £9 billion social housing subsidy has gone on supporting households that are not White British. The Greater London Authority recently revealed that of those households moving into general needs social housing nearly three-quarters – 74% – were headed by someone of Black, Asian, or other minority ethnicity, even though only half of London households are from those groups.

The 2021 census showed that 48% of all social housing in London has gone to households that are headed by somebody who was not born in Britain, with the cost of subsidising these homes to the British taxpayer estimated to be roughly £6 billion a year.

That figure – of foreign-born households living in taxpayer-funded social housing – is also much higher in specific parts of the city. It is 75% in Southall, 72% in places like Haringey and Wembley, 65% in trendy neighbourhoods like Shoreditch and 61% in Bethnal Green. These are prime areas of the city, where young British families and professionals are routinely priced out of the housing market.

Many of the immigrants in social housing are also very recent arrivals. According to official data, roughly a third of London's social housing is occupied by those who only came to Britain between 1991 and 2021, with many long-term British nationals pushed out.

While some immigrant populations – from Western Europe, China and India – occupy social housing at a significantly lower rate than native Britons, for other groups it is a very different story. According to the census, rates of residence in social housing in London exceeded 40% for people born in Bangladesh, Jamaica and many African states such as Nigeria and Ghana. Topping the table at a staggering 74% was Somalia. By comparison, those born in the United Kingdom had a rate of 23%.

Across London, the conclusion is clear: the New Elite have put people from outside our country in front of the people who actually built this country. It is further evidence of a point I have already made: a national welfare system built in the twentieth century to support struggling British citizens has morphed into an international welfare system that today prioritises anybody who is 'in need', no matter where they are from in the world.

That, too, is suicidal empathy in action: a morality in which it is somehow more virtuous to help a stranger from abroad than to honour the obligations owed to one's own people.

Foreign nationals who only arrived in recent years – sometimes illegally – and who often come from radically different cultures, are routinely put ahead of the British people.

Welfare systems and nation-states will only work so long as the people who contribute and pay taxes remain willing to support others they respect and trust, because they know this generosity will be returned by their fellow citizens should they ever need it.

But what happens when the hard-working, tax-paying British majority are instead put in the position of being forced to fund an international welfare regime that actively prioritises strangers who they do not know and who often do not share their language or identity?

Each day, countless British people commute into London from the periphery, travelling on punitively expensive but reliably filthy trains, staring out of the window at prime housing that has either been snapped up by global elites who do not even live in Britain, or handed to migrants who were not born here and are often not contributing to it at all.

How is this fair, many of them will be asking themselves? They have a point.

THE DIVERSITY RELIGION

By now, we are all familiar with the buzzword that provides the justification for cleansing London of its White working class.

'Commitment to diversity,' says London's Labour mayor Sadiq Khan, 'is at the very core of our identity as Londoners.'

And nothing could be less diverse than a Cockney.

To get rid of them entirely, however, they need to be written out of the capital's history. This means the ruling class need an alternative history of London. They have one, and it runs like this. London was built by immigrants. For centuries, the city has had a large foreign population. They enrich London in every sense. Our capital has always been a temple to diversity. And that is just how people like it.

This version of history is now widely accepted and aggressively promoted by the ruling class. Does it sound familiar? It should. Because we are fed the same story on a daily basis about Britain as a whole, a story that we have already seen is not true.

Of course, whether it is true or not does not matter to the ruling class. Just keep repeating these stories until everybody believes them and the White working-class are written out of the script.

Khan tells us: 'This city was built by migrants. By refugees.' But London is a 2,000-year-old city. For almost all of that history it was overwhelmingly White. Migration to the city was internal, from other parts of Britain and from Ireland (which, until 1922, was formerly part of the UK). Khan is also clear about the reasons for London's prosperity: 'It is an uncomfortable truth that our nation and city owes a large part of its wealth to its role in the slave trade.'

Some Londoners would prefer their mayor to focus on old-fashioned things like law and order. Low-level crime in the city is now endemic. Shoplifting is up more than 50% in a year. There is now an unavoidable sense in London that crime pays.

In 2024, just one in every twenty violent muggings were solved. For so-called 'snatch thefts' – where a criminal grabs something from you and makes a getaway – it was even worse. Just one in every 170 such crimes were solved. It is no surprise that 117,000 smartphones were stolen in 2024. These criminals often live in social housing in wealthy parts of London, paid for by British taxpayers, and then repay that generosity by preying on the very people who drive London's wealth and prosperity.

But London's criminality goes beyond theft. Offences involving knives have surged by 60% in three years to record levels. Gangs of young men and children – usually first- or second-generation migrants – murder one another in cold blood.

Shockingly, there is now one alleged rape every hour in a city, where 40% of women feel unsafe walking at night in their own neighbourhood. Yet still elites repeat: 'London is the greatest city in the world.'

So, what are the Metropolitan Police, under Khan's leadership, doing about this? Not much. Instead of making London safer, it is back to gesture politics. The mayor has championed a pointless £6.2 million rebranding exercise that saw London Overground train lines renamed in honour of immigrant communities, an AIDS hospice and the England Women's football team. He had also launched deranged attacks on working people who oppose the expansion of the unpopular 'Ultra Low Emissions Zone' to outer London.

Many residents in outer boroughs with older cars now have to pay £12.50 a day to drive them into these zones. In language that is characteristic of the New Elite, Khan dismissed them as being 'in coalition with the far right'. If you oppose Net Zero measures that are putting a huge burden on hard-working people you are, once again, lumped in with 'the far right'.

In a show of admirable sensitivity towards the hundreds of thousands of people in London who cannot be bothered to learn English, the mayor also instructed his staff not to use the term 'non-English speakers', on the grounds that it 'positions them as flawed and defective'. The preferred term? 'Londoners with English Language Needs'.

Shamefully, Khan has also downplayed the significance of rape gangs in London – or at least quibbled about how to define them. Yet in 2025 it was revealed that the Metropolitan Police are said to be reviewing 9,000 such cases.

The same grim pattern is emerging in London as elsewhere: the authorities blame vulnerable, White working-class children themselves, often in the care system, for being raped and sexually assaulted while frontline politicians turn a blind eye.

During the Covid pandemic, Chris Wild, an author and campaigner who managed six children's care homes across north London in Enfield, Tottenham and Haringey, warned: 'They were losing 50 to 75% of their children every single week to prostitution,' he said. 'It's not as bad as it is in Rotherham, it's worse … We've got a problem in every area of London.'

It may yet turn out, then, that the biggest rape gang cover-up of all time occurred right under the noses of the New Elite, in their celebrated London.

And there are no prizes for guessing why. As we have seen, the elites often think it too incendiary to investigate certain crimes and communities. They would rather turn a blind eye to horrific abuse than risk being called 'racist' or 'Islamophobic', or draw attention to anything that might lead people to question 'diversity'.

That, again, is suicidal empathy: protecting the feelings of abusers over the safety of abused children. Instead of protecting the vulnerable, London's police have been turned into an openly political subdivision of the New Elite, complete with rainbow insignia and 'diversity training'. Despite a budget shortfall, in 2025 the Metropolitan Police still found a way to increase spending on a 'Culture, Diversity and Inclusion Unit', to around £5.2 million.

The force even produced a calendar encouraging the celebration of such key dates as World Hijab Day in February and International Pronouns Day in October. And let us not forget a full seven days for National Tsunami Awareness Week. Perhaps London's police were just so busy caring about all these worthy causes they forgot to investigate the city's rape gangs.

THE DELIVEROO ECONOMY

People who love to sing London's praises will often boast that you can get any type of food in the world delivered to your door in under an hour. And it is true. If that is your metric for a successful society, then London is right up there. But then again, there is also a good chance your takeaway will be delivered by an illegal migrant.

A freedom of information request forced the Home Office to reveal that, during spot checks in 2023, police found that 42% of riders were working illegally. A frequently exploited loophole involves Deliveroo workers – they are not deemed employees – renting out their accounts to people who have no right to work in this country.

Nothing serious is done to stop this, and it is just one area where London's economy offers ample employment for people who are breaking our laws. Others include restaurant kitchens, car washes, construction work and cleaning.

Again, it is worth remembering how many illegal migrants might be in London – about 500,000. That is a city's worth. It would rival Liverpool as the seventh largest city in the country.

Instead of controlling the borders and deporting them, the Labour government suggests that digital identification will fix the problem. This is a fantasy. Digital ID will do little because these jobs are in the 'grey economy', and workers are paid cash in hand.

The truth is that the only way to stop this is for Britain to rebuild its borders.

Anyone who regularly orders Deliveroo in London will have noticed that most riders are from abroad. It should not need saying, but no one should be coming to Britain simply to deliver takeaways. That is not a sign of economic success.

Another increasingly popular job in London's gig economy is working as a private hire driver. With the rise of Uber, there are now around 106,000 such drivers registered in the capital, compared with only 37,000 in 2005. There are, by comparison, fewer than 15,000 black-cab drivers.

I am not criticising the immigrants themselves. I am criticising successive governments, both Labour and Tory, that have deliberately engineered the transformation of our capital.

The big winner in all this is big business – Uber, ride-sharing apps and takeaway apps like Just Eat and Deliveroo. Any hospitality business will be delighted with the endless supply of migrant workers they can pay a pittance.

For London as a whole, however, this project makes zero economic sense. The city's productivity and prosperity are being submerged by the low-skill, low-wage, non-European immigration that, as we have already seen, is a drain on the economy.

It is a serious hit to living standards, with the White British pushed further out by migrants who are more prepared to live in shocking and squalid conditions that more closely resemble the Third World than a modern, civilised state.

The mismatch between the cost of rent and wages is now so great that we are witnessing the return of Dickensian slum landlords. In Brent, a court in 2023 found a man named Jaydipkumar Rameshchandra Valand guilty of putting forty tenants into a four-bedroom property. In Harrow, in 2018, eighteen people were discovered living in a two-bedroom property. In Tower Hamlets, in 2023, Aminur Rahman and his wife Sofina Begum were fined after a three-room flat that they had rented to twenty-two people went up in flames.

One resident, Mizanur Rahman, who had a wife and two children back in Bangladesh, died of smoke inhalation. The cause of the fire was a faulty lithium-ion battery for an e-bike – an essential piece of kit for those working in the Deliveroo economy.

In Newham, Ilyas Patel was fined for letting a four-bedroom property with a severe rodent infestation to four different families, comprising thirteen people in total. Newham Council suspects there may be 6,000 homes within its limits being secretly let to more than one family. If this is what it takes to stay in London, you can understand why the Cockneys left.

This is what suicidal empathy looks like in practice: a capital city that congratulates itself on compassion while building a low-wage, semi-legal underclass and willingly pricing its own people out of the place they built.

'WE'RE ON THE SAME SIDE!'

The policies of mass immigration and two-tier multiculturalism – clamping down on the majority while celebrating minorities – have not only ensured the replacement of the White working-class; they are also entrenching a dark, new sectarianism within the capital. It is a tribalism that would look more at home amid the Troubles in Northern Ireland or the civil strife in Lebanon than in England.

It became visible to everyone in late 2025, when one part of London – Whitechapel, in Tower Hamlets – suddenly captured global attention. In a shameful episode ignored by mainstream media, aggressive groups of Muslim men began patrolling the streets of Whitechapel. They wore black, pulled hoods over their faces and carried baseball bats.

They chanted 'Allahu Akbar' (God is great). They waved the flags of Bangladesh and Palestine. There was not a single woman in sight, nor any hint of loyalty to Britain.

They claimed to be demonstrating their opposition to a

planned protest by a right-wing party. Police rerouted the protest, preventing the party from going anywhere near Whitechapel.

The left's useful idiots were in tow, including the extreme left-wing group Stand Up to Racism. In a telling exchange, one left-wing protestor appealed to one of the masked Muslim men by saying: 'We're on the same side!' The immediate response from one of the masked Muslims was highly symbolic: 'No, we're not,' he shouted back.

The message was clear. It does not matter that this is Britain. The streets of Whitechapel belong to the menacing masked Muslim men. The fascist Blackshirts that had once marched through east London, terrorising locals, it seems, were back; only this time they are Islamists.

The New Elite ignore all this, of course. For them, east London is a shining example of their mantra 'diversity is a success'. Yet if you look past the Whitechapel tube sign translated into Bengali, you will find an area where the full effects of demographic replacement and sectarianism are visible to anyone prepared to look.

Like many other parts of London, more people in Whitechapel were born in the Middle East, Asia, Africa and other regions than were born in Britain. More than one in four residents do not speak English as their main language. More than one in three refuse to take on a British or English identity. Not even one in five are Christian. Only one in three are White. Close to half the population are Muslim.

This is a place that reveals what the social contract in Britain has become – a country where first- or second-generation migrants who often do not contribute are rewarded while British people who do contribute are pushed to the very margins.

Nearly two-thirds of all social housing in this part of London – 64% – has gone to families that are headed by somebody who was not even born in the country. Are they working and contributing to the economy? Only a little over half of them are.

In Tower Hamlets, two-thirds of Muslim households live in social housing. So we have a terrifying show of force from masked Muslim men chanting 'Zionist scum off our streets', with the bill for this intimidation picked up by British taxpayers.

Politics here is no longer about a shared national 'we' but about rival demographic blocs competing for territory, resources and status – the inevitable endpoint when a ruling class treats demographic change as a moral good and national unity as merely an afterthought.

It was also in Tower Hamlets, of course, that Shamima Begum decided in 2015, along with two other girls, to skip school and join Islamic State.

The area's politics tell their own story. Tower Hamlets is one of five authorities in London that elects its own mayor. Bangladesh-born Lutfur Rahman was the Labour mayor before being booted out in 2015, when a court found that he had bribed Bangladeshi and Somali organisations with council grants in exchange for votes.

Rahman also got local imams to tell worshippers it was their duty as Muslims to vote for him. Leaflets and sermons warned Muslims it would be sinful not to do so. Rahman was banned from office for five years. He left Labour and started his own party, Aspire. Today, he is mayor of Tower Hamlets once more.

His voting base, organised along sectarian lines, is simply too strong. Tribal loyalties are too entrenched. Meanwhile, two serving members of Tower Hamlets council decided in 2025 to campaign to become MPs – in Bangladesh.

One of them, Sabina Khan, was a no-show at half the council meetings she was expected at, but she was spotted on social media 5,000 miles away campaigning in Bangladesh. This was yet another example of the dark new sectarianism taking hold of the capital city.

LONDONISTAN

The city's welcoming embrace extends even to those who hate us and want to destroy our country. As early as the 1990s, London was harbouring so many terrorists that French security forces came up with a new nickname for it: Londonistan.

In another classic expression of suicidal empathy, the British state has thrown money at people who hate everything about us – our values, our culture, our country.

Consider Muhammad Qassem Sawalha, allegedly a leading fundraiser for Hamas, the extremist Islamist group that murdered and raped 1,200 Jews in October 2023.

Despite the BBC *Panorama* television programme suggesting that Sawalha had 'masterminded much of Hamas' political and military strategy', he was still allowed to settle in Britain and given social housing, once again paid for by the British people.

British taxpayers did not just fund his social housing; they helped him buy his property through a Right to Buy scheme, including a discount of £112,300, and for good measure made him a British citizen. Homes for British families? Not a chance. Homes for Hamas? Absolutely.

Nor is this the only example of the British people being forced to subsidise foreigners who hate Britain and the British people. Take the four-man Islamic State terrorist cell their captives nicknamed 'the Beatles' on account of their English accents. These Beatles were not Scousers. All four grew up in that very place elites tell us is a beacon of diversity: London.

The group was active in Syria and Iraq, but appeared on screens around the world in grisly videos of the beheading of victims including the aid workers David Haines and Alan Henning. Even by Islamic State's standards, they were notorious for their brutality – torturing victims and subjecting them to mock executions. They made James Foley, an American journalist, endure a pretend crucifixion.

The most vicious member, Mohammed Emwazi, was nicknamed 'Jihadi John'. Before joining Islamic State, Emwazi and his family had been subsidised by the British people, living in social housing on the Mozart Estate in Queen's Park, where more than half of all social housing has gone to households headed by somebody who was not even born in Britain.

Another extremist funded by the British people is Egyptian al-Qaeda hate preacher Hani al-Sibai. He was suspected of radicalising Jihadi John, as well as the group that recruited a gunman who murdered thirty British tourists in Tunisia in 2015.

He praised the 7/7 al-Qaeda suicide bombings in London, which killed fifty-two people, as 'a great victory'. In 2005, the US

Treasury accused him of 'training and providing material support to al-Qaida, as well as conspiring to commit terrorist acts'.

Nonetheless, the British state still handed him a cosy three-storey, four-bedroom home in leafy Ravenscourt Park, worth around £1 million, a neighbourhood where half of all social housing has gone to people who were not even born in Britain. He and his wife also pocketed some £48,000 a year in welfare benefits – again, paid for by British taxpayers.

My critics will say I am cherry-picking cases. But I could go on for a very long time. What about the hook-handed Islamist preacher Abu Hamza? He, too, was treated to a huge five-bedroom house in Shepherd's Bush, west London, along with welfare benefits of £33,000 a year for his wife and children, all while he radicalised young Muslims at Finsbury Park Mosque, urging them to attack Britain and the West.

So, too, was Omar Bakri Muhammad, the Syrian-born extremist cleric who became known as the 'Tottenham Ayatollah'. Despite celebrating the 9/11 terror attacks, creating the extremist group Al-Muhajiroun, calling for an Islamic state under Sharia law, and branding Britain 'Dar al-Kufr' – the land of unbelievers – he was given a council house in Tottenham and welfare benefits. Yet another man who returned the British people's generosity by using the free speech and welfare they gave him to call for the destruction of their country.

Hate preacher Anjem Choudary even claimed housing benefit from the state to pay his own father-in-law, whose mortgage-free house he lived in with his wife. Choudary described the 9/11 terrorists as 'magnificent martyrs' and encouraged his own followers to claim what he called 'jihad-seeker's allowance'. He justified the claiming of benefits by saying: 'The money belongs to Allah and if it is given, you can take it.'

Counter-terrorism sources said that Choudary influenced more than one hundred British jihadis. One of his followers was Michael Adebolajo, one of the two Londoners who murdered and beheaded off-duty British soldier Lee Rigby in Woolwich in 2013.

'We have harboured those who hated us', wrote Margaret Thatcher, in the shadow of the 9/11 Islamist attacks. 'Tolerated those who threatened us and indulged those who weakened us'. Thatcher was absolutely right then, and she is right now. Look around London and you will find countless examples of the ruling class harbouring, if not prioritising, newcomers and outsiders who hate us, threaten us and weaken us – all in the name of a warped, suicidal understanding of empathy. The same mentality that allowed Pakistani Muslim rape gangs to operate for years now hands social housing, welfare, even passports to men who praise suicide bombings and dream of the destruction of our entire civilisation.

A BETTER LONDON

You will remember how New Labour calculated that immigrants would be more likely to vote for them – and that was as good a reason as any to open the floodgates. It was a cynical calculation that has been proven correct in London, at least for now.

The city has a Labour mayor, and the party dominated the capital at the 2024 general election. In Inner London, which has seen much higher immigration, Labour won a clean sweep of seats, with the exception of Islington, which went to Jeremy Corbyn, an independent.

It is worth remembering that it was not just Labour that did this to our capital. The Tories made every effort to keep big business happy by keeping the taps of mass immigration turned on. As Mayor of London (2008–16), Boris Johnson even called for an amnesty for illegal immigrants if they had been in Britain for four years – at a time when there was an estimated 400,000 in the capital.

That is nothing, however, compared with Labour mayor Sadiq Khan, who has called for London to be able to set its own immigration policy separate from the rest of the country. How that would ever work is anyone's guess.

It was Labour who really began the project of demographic replacement. And despite everything our capital city has suffered, there are still many in the party unashamed to claim responsibility. The verdict of one New Labour insider, John McTernan, who briefly served as Tony Blair's political secretary, was simply: 'A better London has been created'.

And there you have the New Elite's view in a nutshell: fewer White British people in London, and in Britain, is a good thing. The demographic replacement of the White British is to be celebrated and cheered on. This is what 'diversity' really means in their new religion – protecting and promoting every group, except the one that happened to build the country.

Londoners can sense that the social contract is fraying.

Everyone is increasingly in it for themselves. You can feel the difference. People are becoming harder and more selfish.

I used to love our capital city, but today it is hard to escape the conclusion that London has fallen. It has been betrayed by elites who celebrate the demise of the city's native inhabitants and congratulate themselves for doing so in the name of empathy, inclusion and diversity.

London shows us what happens when all the forces I have described in this book are left to run unchecked. Mass legal immigration and broken borders changed who lives in the capital. Two-tier multiculturalism has changed whose side the state takes. The censorship regime makes it dangerous to complain. And over all of it, suicidal empathy told the elite that dismantling their own majority was not just acceptable, but virtuous.

The rest of the country should sit up and take note. What happens when the people of a country are barely visible at all in their capital city, in the place that is meant to symbolise that country? What will remain of our old capital when – as has already happened in boroughs like Brent and Newham – the historic majority falls below 20%?

How can a capital city even be the capital of a nation if the people who built that nation are no longer present? And are people across Britain sufficiently willing to resist their demographic replacement in a way the people of London were not able to do?

Those are the questions that will decide whether London is a warning or simply the first part of Britain to fall.

CHAPTER EIGHT

HOW TO SAVE THE COUNTRY

The fall of a country is never the work of a single moment. No one event, no one disaster, no matter how severe or catastrophic, can overthrow an entire people. Not invasion. Not disease. Not sheer misfortune.

Long before the final collapse, something inside the civilisation has already begun to decay. The seeds of ruin are sown long before the moment comes to pass – and invariably they are often sown by the very people who were entrusted with its protection.

Every civilisation that collapses first suffers a withdrawal of belief among its leaders. They may not openly declare that their inheritance is no longer worth defending, but their actions or indifference reveal the truth to the people they are supposed to serve.

Whatever faith they had – in the country, in its people, in the future – they either misplaced or surrendered. Either way, it is the elites – not the immigrants, asylum seekers and refugees – who end up calling time on the life of a country.

When those who are supposed to be guarding the gates cease to care whether the gates remain standing at all, things begin to unravel slowly at first – and then all at once. What once seemed unshakeable rapidly starts to unravel. What once felt eternal suddenly appears fragile. And what once made a country special and unique quickly fades from view.

This is what is now unfolding in Britain, for all the reasons we have explored in this book: the relentless tide of mass legal immigration, broken borders, two-tier multiculturalism and, most of all, a ruling class that is willing to destroy its own country in the name of showing compassion to others. Even if the elites deny it, millions of people can feel it.

TWO PATHS

Britain now stands at a fork in the road. The choice the country must make will determine whether it continues as a distinctive nation-state that is anchored in a historic majority, or disappears into something that is unrecognisable from all that we have known.

This choice cannot be kicked into the long grass. The reason I wrote this book is because the people must decide – *now* – or they will lose the right to choose their own destiny.

One path leads us onward in the same direction that we have travelled for the past thirty reckless years. It is the path of suicidal empathy – a path defined by the abandonment of self-belief, the elevation of abstract compassion for outsiders ahead of duty to our own people, and the refusal to recognise the dire effects of mass uncontrolled immigration, rapid demographic change and the grim fate that awaits the historic majority as it slides into minority status.

By now, having explored the evidence that I have shared in this book, we know precisely where that path will lead us: to fragmentation, sectarianism, segregation, instability, division and relentless chaos, if not the eventual collapse of our country.

The other path is older. Straighter. More demanding. It is the path that is unfashionable in elite circles in the BBC or Westminster but is the one that our ancestors walked.

It is the path of patriotism, duty and faith. This path asks that we show compassion and loyalty first and foremost to our own people. It puts the historic majority of people who built Britain – unequivocally and unapologetically first.

We are told we should not walk that path. It is smeared as 'dangerous' and 'divisive' by the very people who have imposed a dangerous experiment on the country and divided our communities. With no democratic mandate, they have imposed the most dramatic social, cultural and demographic transformation in our country's history.

It took place not over centuries, nor even over generations, but within the span of only thirty years – not even half a lifetime. Nothing like it has happened before on these islands. Yet here we are.

This revolution was engineered by a ruling class who neither sought nor cared about consent from the people. At no point were the taxpaying citizens of this country allowed to vote on it. They were never asked about it. When they protested, they were patronised, ignored and pathologised.

The consequences have been profound and, unless we urgently change course, will soon be irreversible. The White British will become a minority among young people by the middle of this century and a minority overall in less than forty years. In less than a lifetime one-third of all young people on these islands could soon be following Islam.

The demographic foundations that have supported our country for centuries are now collapsing with astonishing speed and yet nobody in Westminster is even willing to talk about it. This is why I wrote this book. I knew that I would be attacked for writing it.

Yet I wanted to tell you – the people – what is happening in your own country. What I have shared with you are not speculative claims. They are reliable projections based on official statistics from the very institutions and authorities our elites revere.

And still, knowing what lies ahead, our rulers refuse to speak honestly and openly with you. They keep this information hidden from the very people they have been elected to serve. Why? Because honesty would expose their project. It would undo them. They cannot admit this is the outcome they desire – the permanent, irreversible transformation of Britain – because they know the people would recoil and threaten their power.

And so they proceed in silence. Through omission. Through deception. Through obfuscation. Through the erosion of truth. And while practising the very thing they accuse others of: 'misinformation'. They constantly gaslight, mislead and confuse the very people whose interests they are supposed to defend and represent.

What is now unfolding in Britain is not simply demographic change. It is not the natural rhythm and flow of a country's population. It is civilisational transformation – or what the United States warned European nations they now face in the final days of 2025: 'civilisational erasure' – the looming disappearance of their special and unique identity, culture and people.

When the historic ethnic and cultural core of a nation greatly weakens or even disappears, that nation cannot continue as before. It becomes something else entirely: a territory with institutions but without a shared cultural inheritance, without a collective memory of itself and without any meaningful sense of belonging.

Call it whatever you want, but it will no longer be a nation in the way that our ancestors understood that word. Such a country may survive as a bland administrative unit, but it will not survive as a nation, as a home, with a distinctive identity, culture, history and way of life.

It might call itself Britain. It might bear a passing resemblance to Britain. But it will not *be* Britain.

And so here we stand, at a historic crossroads that our ancestors never imagined, facing truths that once felt too impolite to say but are now too obvious to ignore, and experiencing feelings of profound loss and dispossession that we would rather ignore yet know that we cannot. Before this decade ends, we will either reclaim our future or we will lose it.

A LOSS OF FAITH

How did we arrive here? How did a once-confident and proud nation allow itself to drift into a future it never chose to begin with? The answer, as I have stressed, is not the immigrants, asylum seekers and refugees who are arriving in huge numbers, legally or illegally. It is about those who govern us. It is a story of relentless disappointment and, yes, betrayal.

For the past thirty years, it has not mattered who occupied Number 10 Downing Street. Whether left or right, Labour or Tory, a succession of governments have imposed a single, suffocating project on the rest of the country: that Britain must be totally transformed through mass immigration and rapid demographic change and that this was both inevitable and desirable.

The New Elite joined together to celebrate the same dreary project: a nation subjected to relentless change, its borders blurred and prised open, its historic majority diminished, its culture, traditions and history treated as an embarrassment.

On the green benches in the House of Commons, implicitly encouraging the demographic replacement of the historic majority group in this country has become not a scandal but a symbol of elite sophistication.

No matter who the prime minister happens to be, the result for the people is always the same – higher numbers, faster change, less control, no matter the consequences.

Every prime minister, from Tony Blair to David Cameron, Boris Johnson to Keir Starmer, has disappointed more than the last. Their promises have dissolved into nothing. The direction has never changed or slowed. At every election, the British people have been told 'this time will be different', only to then watch the same project not only continue but accelerate even faster. It has been an unending catalogue of dashed hopes and deep disillusionment, an extended betrayal by Westminster that has shattered public trust and confidence in democracy, divided our country, and put us firmly on course towards chaos and carnage.

Behind all the politicians stands the same entrenched network: civil servants, unelected officials, state bureaucrats, media executives, judges, corporate leaders, academics and more.

The New Elite, united not by class or income but by ideology. United in their desire to remake Britain into something its own people never wanted. United in their insistence that anybody who resists their extreme project is somehow backward, illegitimate, or immoral.

And united in a worldview that is not rooted in what our country's leaders used to value – duty, service, national loyalty – but in suicidal empathy: an insidious, dangerous moral instinct that equates national self-preservation with moral failure. True virtue, today's leaders believe, lies not in protecting their own people but in sacrificing them on the altar of showing empathy to outsiders and foreigners.

Yet while they claim these things, what they practise in reality is contempt – contempt for Britain's borders, contempt for democracy, contempt for the people whose lives they are transforming without consent, contempt for the idea that a nation belongs to its citizens not its rulers, and contempt for the historic majority, for the very idea people have a right to exist.

Again, immigrants pursuing their own interests are not to blame for any of this. The people I blame are those in Westminster who rule over us.

The blame belongs squarely to the ruling class that allowed this to happen, that ignored the warnings, and have abandoned their responsibility to conserve the nation. They have withdrawn completely from the very people they claim to represent, turning inwards and away from the nation. Our leaders have lost faith in Britain and so the people have lost faith in them, pushing us further towards civil unrest.

This is no longer just a warning. Increasingly, serious scholars of civil war and strategy are sounding the alarm about the direction of travel. Professor David Betz, one of Britain's leading authorities on conflict and state fragility, argues that Western nations like Britain are rapidly drifting into – if they are not already in it – what he calls a condition of 'post-sovereign disorder': a state in which authority erodes, rival group identities harden and parallel societies take root.

In these circumstances, Betz warns, countries do not slide neatly into a formal civil war of the kind we might recognise from history books. Rather, they enter long periods of chronic instability – spasms of sectarian tension, episodic violence and the fracturing and eventual collapse of the social contract, much of which we can now already see playing out in parts of Britain – from intergroup tensions on the streets of Leicester to widespread rioting in the aftermath of the atrocities in Southport, from the kind of tribal displays we explored in Whitechapel to growing evidence of Islamic sectarianism in British politics.

Betz's key insight is both clear and profoundly unsettling: a toxic combination of suicidal empathy and demographic replacement has not only weakened Britain's borders and institutions, it has weakened the country itself. A nation that can no longer enforce its laws, define its identity, or secure the trust of its own citizens becomes highly vulnerable not to invasion from without, but to disintegration from within.

Betz does not say this future is inevitable. But he does show, through his rigorous research, that the conditions for serious internal conflict are already present in Britain, and that our leaders' refusal to confront reality is accelerating the danger.

If we do not act now, the next stage of decline will not just be cultural loss. It will be social fragmentation, unrest and the return of forces that our ancestors spent centuries suppressing. And even worse: it will have been brought upon us by our own leaders.

AMONG THE WRECKAGE

The elites will either attack or ignore this book. But its contents – the consequences of their failing project – have now become impossible to ignore.

They surround us on all sides. Public trust has collapsed. Social cohesion has frayed. Entire neighbourhoods have been utterly transformed beyond recognition in only a few years.

Public services buckle under the weight of unprecedented demand. Welfare costs surge. Housing costs soar. Imported conflicts spill out onto once calm British streets. Sectarian tensions reshape politics in Westminster. Extremists openly mock the nation that gives them refuge.

The British people now look out and see an impotent state that is unable to deport foreign criminals and illegal migrants and keep their own people safe. Extremist Islamists preach hate against Britain while at the same time being subsidised by the very people they yearn to destroy – a classic marker of suicidal empathy if ever there was one.

A unified nation is dissolving into competing groups that are being pushed apart by the state, encouraged to cultivate their own identities, while the majority is urged to abandon its identity and treated as inherently problematic and threatening.

London, our capital, now feels like a foreign city – a symbol of the demographic trends that will soon sweep through the rest of the country. Two-tier multiculturalism demands everything from the White British majority but nothing from the minorities it considers sacred and virtuous. It praises diversity while dismantling national unity. It places the language of rights and diversity above the obligations of citizenship. It celebrates difference while eroding belonging. And it endlessly lectures the majority of people who built this country while excusing the failures of newcomers, even when they harm our own people.

And while all this is happening, the state grows ever larger: Big Welfare, Big Debt, Big Tax, Big Spending, Big Immigration, Big Net Zero, Big Censorship – big on everything except the virtues that once made Britain bloom: individual freedom, hard work, entrepreneurship, free speech, aspiration, controlled borders, stability, manageable change.

Elites have turned Britain into a place that is now fully addicted to mass immigration while more than four million British people live on out-of-work benefits with no requirement to look for work, and a million young Brits are not in education, employment, or training.

And still the New Elite insist on importing more migrant labour rather than investing in their own people. They are failing, put simply, to look after their own.

Unsurprisingly, many who can afford to do so have started to leave Britain altogether. In 2025, net emigration of British people rivalled the number of asylum seekers arriving. This is not renewal, this is demographic replacement. When a country allows masses of non-European migrants to essentially replace its own, that country has visibly given up.

All of it was avoidable. Suicidal empathy took hold and blinded our ruling class to everything except their own narcissistic need to feel morally superior. So long as they were applauded in newspaper columns, company boardrooms and dinner parties for the BBC and Westminster set, the consequences for the country were considered irrelevant. They insulated themselves from the chaos and carnage they unleashed: private schools, expensive neighbourhoods, gated estates and – like Boris Johnson – literal moats.

They imposed this demographic revolution on everybody else while protecting themselves from it. You will never find them in the places they have transformed beyond all recognition. They are always somewhere else, leaving it to the less fortunate to have to navigate the effects of their disastrous decisions.

WHAT MUST NOW BE DONE

If Britain is to be saved from this fragmentation, instability and eventual civilisational suicide, it must change course immediately.

The measures that are required are not extreme, far from it. They are the minimum for national continuity. Those who led our nation until 1997 would consider them common sense.

To begin with, we need a full moratorium on immigration – an immediate end to the policy of mass uncontrolled immigration that is making us poorer, more divided and shattering the foundations of our democracy.

We must follow the example of the United States in the 1920s by passing laws to drastically reduce legal immigration and give our country, our culture and our people a chance to recover from the enormous damage of the last thirty years.

We must fully end Britain's dependence on low-wage, low-skill migration from outside Europe – a model that depresses wages, undercuts British workers, puts unprecedented strains on housing and reshapes the country around people who do not share our culture. The days of importing millions of people who are not only a net drain on the economy but come from radically different cultures must end.

This means withdrawing the right for the millions of migrants who have arrived in Britain since 2019 – as part of the Boriswave – to qualify for 'Indefinite Leave to Remain', securing the right to remain in the country for ever and enjoy welfare benefits, student loans and the ability to bring more of their relatives into Britain.

Nobody voted for this demographic change. Nobody asked for it. Nobody wants to have an estimated bill of roughly £200 billion, if not more, imposed on the British people. Only the elites desire it.

We must also rebuild our borders and restore full national sovereignty. No nation can survive if it cannot decide who can enter and who must leave. No nation can control its borders if it does not control its laws. That means leaving – not just reforming – the European Convention on Human Rights and repealing the Human Rights Act, which together place decisions about our country in the hands of activist lawyers and foreign judges.

It means immediately disapplying any law or international convention that prevents us from controlling our own borders and putting the interests of our own people where they belong: first. This will allow us to disempower a remote, unaccountable and self-serving class of activist lawyers who now routinely put international human rights before the rights of our national citizens. Such as prioritising the rights of Afghan asylum seeker Lawangeen Abdulrahimzai, who told British authorities he was fourteen when in fact he was nineteen and had already shot two men to death in Serbia. He was then placed in a school alongside British children, before murdering Thomas Roberts in Bournemouth in March 2022.

Or prioritising the rights of small-boat migrant Amin Abedi Mofrad, a thirty-five-year-old Iranian who, despite being convicted of eleven offences in Germany, was still allowed into Britain, where he raped a fifteen-year-old girl in Oxford. As her mother asked the Home Office: why are these people allowed into our country in the first place?

Leaving the ECHR, overhauling the laws that are weakening our country, will allow us to detain and deport anybody who enters illegally – without apology. Your first act on entering a country cannot be to break the law. Putting the rights of illegal migrants before the rights of your own people is how leaders tear apart the social contract.

It will also make it easier to deport foreign criminals, while the government should use foreign aid and visa penalties to ensure that countries accept the migrants we are returning.

Citizens who are forced to subsidise illegal migrants and the growing costs of extreme policies they never voted for will inevitably withdraw their support for the welfare state and perhaps even democracy itself. This is the path our leaders are now pushing us down.

We must also process claims for asylum offshore – in a safe third country – away from the hardworking, law-abiding, taxpaying majority. This will reduce incentives for migration and allow us to redirect the billions of pounds that are currently being spent on people breaking our laws into frontline services such as the police and the NHS.

The ruling class will shriek that leaving the European Convention on Human Rights would 'turn us into Russia and Belarus', who are also not members. This is nonsense. In reality, it would simply align us with many other advanced nations around the world – the United States, Canada, Australia, New Zealand and much of the Commonwealth – that do not adhere to the ECHR and subject their people to the consequent harm.

We must overturn two-tier multiculturalism and replace it with a far more assertive state policy of assimilation. Our country cannot continue to tell newcomers they should retain their distinctive identities and cultures while telling the historic majority to jettison theirs. The days of tolerating people who hate who we are must end.

Newcomers must adopt the language, norms and obligations of British society. They must also be expected to make a net contribution to the economy.

Parallel legal and cultural systems should be abolished. Sharia councils must be banned. Cousin marriage must be prohibited. The burqa, niqab and other forms of religious dress should no longer be permitted in public spaces.

Translation services in public institutions must end. Diversity, equality and inclusion policies must be stripped out of taxpayer-funded institutions. They divide people, erode national loyalty and stigmatise the majority.

The British people should no longer be forced to pay an estimated £10 billion a year providing welfare support to more than 1.2 million foreign nationals, and another £6 billion subsidising social housing for foreign-born households.

Nor should they continue to pay more than £10 billion a year in foreign aid until they have well-functioning healthcare, educational and criminal justice systems of their own. The absurdity of forcing the British people to subsidise much of the rest of the world while having to live without functioning public services of their own must end. How is it right that people are forced to do this while some of them are being treated in hospital corridors?

Our national ethos must once again be national preference. British families first in housing. British workers first in employment. British citizens first in welfare. British identity first in the public realm.

The ruling class will tell you that these steps are 'xenophobic' or 'irresponsible', but they are not. They are necessary to ensure the continuity of a nation. Irresponsible is tearing up the social contract and pushing your country towards the abyss. Putting your own people first is not extreme: it is survival.

REPLACING THE NEW ELITE

There is now an unbridgeable gulf between what the people want and what the ruling class is prepared to deliver. This gap cannot be closed by gentle persuasion, private lobbying, or polite requests. For the last thirty years the New Elite have consistently refused to strike a compromise with the people. They have ignored, mocked and gaslit those who pay their salaries. They will never do what needs to be done. The difference between their values and your values is simply too great, which is why they must be removed from power.

For decades, those who have ruled over this country have been able to rely on the patience of our people, even on their lack of interest in politics. The British, after all, have a long history of tolerating mediocre leaders so long as they maintained order and were committed to the continuity of the nation.

G. K. Chesterton captured the mood of the once-patient people when he wrote: 'For we are the people of England, that never have spoken yet.'

But now the people have been pushed to breaking point and are speaking – more loudly each year. They have a simple demand. They want their leaders gone. They want the ruling class of the last thirty years that has failed them removed. The only question is whether the people will succeed, or whether the elites will find, as they have so many times before, some way to cling to authority and power.

And so the defining question of this century is simple: do the British still want Britain to exist? I am not talking about the cli-chés of tea, queueing, apologies and cricket, the platitudes that are wheeled out by the political and media class. I am talking about the nation itself – the culture, the identity, the story, the people, the inheritance.

The country does not belong to the discredited ruling class in Westminster, it belongs to the people. If the people decide that they want Britain to continue in a form they recognise and sup-port, it is they who will need to bring about change.

If they remain silent, much of what we associate with the country will rapidly fade from view. Britain's distinctive identity, culture, history and way of life will all disappear forever.

A civilisation may die in many ways but demographic self-abolition is the most final way. There is no coming back from that. And while it can survive invasion, it cannot survive indifference.

If the people fail to act, the loss will be final – as final as if the island itself were to sink beneath the waves. But if the people do act – if they reclaim what was theirs by correcting the system and forcing through political change – this country may yet rise again. The institutions that imposed this demographic revolution will need to be confronted and overhauled. The underlying ideology that justified it will need to be rejected.

Unless we meet this moment in history directly, we will fail in our promise to our ancestors to pass on the country that we know and love. A proud nation will have undone itself.

The hour is late, but not too late. History shows that the British often take action at the last moment. We stumble, we falter, we waste time – and then, at the very last, we rise.

Britain is not yet dead, but it is in mortal danger. If it is to be saved from suicide, it must be now. The final pages of our civilisation need not be written yet. Not here. Not if the British people refuse to go meekly into the long night of a final, deadly decline. Not if they decide that this home, this inheritance, this country is worth fighting for.

The choice remains ours.

References

1   More In Common poll. Available online: https://www.moreincommon.org.uk/blog/social-cohesion-a-snapshot/

2   The forecasts are based on the most reliable census data and a statistical technique called the 'cohort-component' approach, a standard technique in the study of populations. See: 'Britain in 2100. My Exclusive Presentation on the Trends Reshaping the Nation', Matt Goodwin's Substack Newsletter. Available at: https://www.mattgoodwin.org/p/britain-in-2100-my-exclusive-presentation?utm_source=publication-search

3   This refers to state-funded schools and nurseries. Schools, pupils, and their characteristics. 5 June 2025. https://explore-education-statistics.service.gov.uk/find-statistics/school-pupils-and-their-characteristics/2024-25

4   White British children are minority at one in four schools, *Daily Telegraph*, 7 June 2025. Available online: https://www.telegraph.co.uk/news/2025/06/07/white-british-children-now-minority-one-in-four-schools/Footnote

5   Data based on a release to Neil O'Brien MP. 'Migration and Ethnicity: Part One', Neil O'Brien's Substack. Available online: https://www.neilobrien.co.uk/p/migration-and-ethnicity-part-one (accessed 17 November 2025).

6   'Wow. Bombshell Numbers Show How Fast the UK Population is Changing', Matt Goodwin's Substack Newsletter. Available online: https://www.mattgoodwin.org/p/wow-bombshell-numbers-show-how-fast?utm_source=publication-search

7   'Europe's Growing Muslim Population', Pew Research Center. Available online: https://www.pewresearch.org/religion/2017/11/29/europes-growing-muslim-population/ (accessed 27 October 2025).

8   'Views on the importance of language and national identity', Pew Research Center, January 18 2024. Available online: https://www.pewresearch.org/global/2024/01/18/views-on-the-importance-of-language-to-national-identity/

9   This refers to state-funded schools and nurseries. Schools, pupils, and their characteristics. 5 June 2025. https://explore-education-statistics.service.gov.uk/find-statistics/school-pupils-and-their-characteristics/2024-25

10 'How a school is beating the odds with music', *BBC News* September 19 2018. Available online: https://www.bbc.com/news/stories-45483930

11 Bell Foundation evidence submitted to parliament, 2023, available online: https://committees.parliament.uk/writtenevidence/122798/pdf/; 'Schools are pocketing up to £700,000 each to teach pupils who don't speak English as their first language as bill hits all-time high of £572 million', *Daily Mail* April 4 2026. Available online: https://www.dailymail.co.uk/news/article-15553095/schools-local-authorities-non-English-speaking-kids-speed.html

12 Matthew J. Goodwin (2023) *Values, Voice, and Virtue: The New British Politics*, Penguin.

13 For a review of this evidence see Matt Goodwin, 'The economic case for mass immigration is collapsing', Matt Goodwin Substack, October 2024, https://www.mattgoodwin.org/p/the-economic-case-for-mass-immigration?utm_source=publication-search (accessed 24 November 2025).

14 Roger Scruton (2004) *The Need for Nations*, Civitas: Institute for the Study of Civil Society.

15 'Foreigners three times as likely to be arrested for sex offences as British citizens', *Daily Telegraph* January 5, 2025. Available online: https://www.telegraph.co.uk/news/2025/01/05/foreign-national-crime-league-table-sexual-offence-migrants/; see also Matt Goodwin, 'Mass immigration is making you less safe: what a shocking new study finds', Matt Goodwin Substack. Available online: https://www.mattgoodwin.org/p/mass-immigration-is-making-you-less

16 'Foreign nationals convicted of quarter of sex assaults on women', *Daily Telegraph*, 18 June 2025. Available online: https://www.telegraph.co.uk/news/2025/06/18/foreign-nationals-convicted-quarter-of-sex-assaults-women/ (accessed 10 November 2025).

17 Francis Fukuyama (2022) *Liberalism and its Discontents*. Profile Books.

18 Matt Goodwin, 'Shocking: What British Muslims Think', Matt Goodwin Substack, April 10 2024. Available online: https://www.mattgoodwin.org/p/shocking-what-british-muslims-think?utm_source=publication-search (accessed January 8 2026).

19 Douglas Murray (2019) *The Madness of Crowds: Gender, Race, and Identity*, Bloomsbury.

20 Matthew J. Goodwin (2025) *Bad Education: Why Our Universities Are Broken and How We Can Fix Them*. Random House.